Berry Benson's
Civil War Book

☆
☆ ☆ ☆

Berry Benson's
Civil War Book

*Memoirs of a Confederate Scout
and Sharpshooter*

☆ ☆ ☆
☆

Edited by

SUSAN WILLIAMS BENSON

Foreword by

HERMAN HATTAWAY

THE UNIVERSITY OF GEORGIA PRESS
ATHENS AND LONDON

Published in 1992 by the
University of Georgia Press, Athens, Georgia 30602
© 1991 by Frances Benson Thompson
Foreword © 1992
by the University of Georgia Press

The paper in this book meets the guidelines for
permanence and durability of the Committee
on Production Guidelines for Book Longevity
of the Council on Library Resources.

Printed in the United States of America

01 00 99 98 97   C   7 6 5 4 3

Library of Congress Cataloging in Publication Data

Benson, Berry, 1843–1923.
    [Civil War book]
    Berry Benson's Civil War book : memoirs of a
Confederate scout and sharpshooter / edited by
Susan Williams Benson ; foreword by Herman Hattaway.
        p.   cm.
    ISBN 0-8203-1487-0 (alk. paper)
    1. Benson, Berry, 1843–1923. 2. United States—
History—Civil War, 1861–1865—Personal narratives,
Confederate. 3. United States—History—Civil War,
1861–1865—Prisoners and prisons. 4. United States—
History—Civil War, 1861–1865—Scouts and scouting.
5. Scouts and scouting—Confederate States of
America—Biography. I. Benson, Susan Williams.
II. Title. III. Title: Civil War book.
E605.B455   1992
973.7'82—dc20   92–27349
                                                    CIP

British Library Cataloging in Publication Data available

Berry Benson's Civil War Book was originally published
in 1962 by the University of Georgia Press, Athens.

To My Husband
CHARLES GREENWOOD BENSON
*in whose memory the editing
of his father's memoirs was
undertaken*

☆ ☆

Contents

FOREWORD   ix

PREFACE   xv

I   A YOUNG VOLUNTEER   1

II   UNDER STONEWALL JACKSON   16

III I MISS GETTYSBURG   41

IV   A SCOUT AND SHARPSHOOTER   57

V   A PRISONER OF THE YANKEES   83

VI   ELMIRA PRISON   126

VII A FUGITIVE IN ENEMY COUNTRY   151

VIII FINAL RESISTANCE   174

☆　☆

Foreword

It has been thirty years since the University of Georgia Press first published this readable and valuable memoir by one of the most remarkable of the Confederate sharpshooters and scouts, Berry Benson. Copies of the printed volume have become rare, and although the original handwritten manuscript has long been available to scholars at the University of North Carolina's Southern Historical Collection, the present army of Civil War enthusiasts should welcome this convenient new edition. Benson was the kind of soldier whose exploits made him fully deserve the statue of him that is part of the Augusta, Georgia, Civil War monument. Along with his wartime achievements, his memoir is truly monumental.

The stuff of which legends are made, Benson was not yet eighteen when he went off to war. He fought all the way: from first Manassas, through the Seven Days' Battles, Sharpsburg, Chancellorsville, the Wilderness, Spotsylvania, and Petersburg, to Appomattox. Rising quickly to the rank of sergeant, on several occasions he commanded his company. He was twice captured, and his daring and thrilling escapes from Union prisons are riveting stories of the first order. He never surrendered. When the last hope evaporated, he simply walked away, returned home, and kept his cherished weapon as a symbol of personal defiance.

Thoroughly dedicated to the southern cause, he endured all manner of hardships—and bore them stoically. His memoir contains no self-pity: not for the physical privation, the body lice, the hard labors of soldier life, nor for the pains of his several wounds. Often food was so scarce that men resorted to shocking expedients. He was fortunate not to have been hungry enough to partake of cooked rat the first time his companions tried it—and assured him (he being content to take their word)—that rat tasted like young squirrel. Later he was not so finicky, and while in Federal prison he ate many a rat. Benson was so keenly aware of how bad things sometimes were that he found it believable—as he was told—that in the field some wretched Confederates had picked grains of corn out of horses' dung, washed them, and cooked them for food. But all of this was, he thought, tribute to the pluck of dedicated fighting men, and he was convinced that soldiers on both sides often endured, in one form or another, equal indignities.

Benson long treasured two particular memories he recalled as "the brightest pictures of the war"; both were instances of valor displayed by enemy officers: one during the Battle at Sharpsburg and the other at first Cold Harbor (during the Seven Days' Battles). In each case, a Union officer had ridden boldly to the front, waving the flag, rallying his faltering men, only to be cut down by withering rifle fire. And while Benson did feel unceasing regret that southerners had to kill such brave men, he never lost faith that it had been their duty to do so, for such "was the most tremendous enemy we had."

Benson learned early that "a battlefield is not a drillroom, nor is battle an occasion for drill." Once engaged, the soldiers discarded drill routines. Veterans relied on each other's instincts. Rank made little difference, and orders might be shouted out by anyone who happened to be standing in the best position to see an advantage. The charge might be initiated by any private who suddenly felt inspiration that the moment had come to spring forward.

The southern soldiers with whom Benson was associated seem generally—like himself—to have had very high morale. His memoir suggests that they grieved much more following the death of Stonewall Jackson than they did over the tragic outcome at Gettysburg. "I have heard men, worn out by a break-neck march, cursing Jackson bitterly," Benson reminisced, "yet all the while they worshipped him, and could not have been bribed to drop out of ranks." As for Gettysburg, though a wound caused him to miss that battle, his brother Blackwood's letters convinced him that "there was not the slightest feeling of defeat amongst the men."

Nearly one-half of Benson's memoir is devoted to his numerous near-captures and the more unfortunate episodes when he did fall captive. Once he escaped from a prison camp near the Potomac River and subsequently experienced some terrifying moments when he encountered sharks in Chesapeake Bay. He almost succeeded that time in getting back to the Confederate army, but in the end he was recaptured and shipped off to one of the more infamous northern prisons, at Elmira, New York.

There, some ten thousand hapless men lived under close guard. Elmira was no pleasant place. Administrators purposefully meted out harsh treatment—in retaliation for deprivations suffered by Federal prisoners in the South. From the outset, medical care at Elmira was poor. Supplies were grossly inadequate. It was a most unsanitary prison; disease was rampant. The 24 percent death rate at Elmira overwhelmingly topped the average 12 percent death rate at the more than 150 other prisons holding Confederate soldiers. The first captives to arrive were housed in thirty-five two-story wooden barracks formerly used by Federal recruits undergoing training, but the buildings were inadequate for wintertime use, and the suffering was intense. Eventually gross overcrowding forced many prisoners—including Benson—to live in tents pitched on the surrounding grounds. "If there was ever a hell on earth," one Texas soldier later asserted, "Elmira prison was that hell."

Benson became involved in several different tunneling attempts aimed at burrowing under a twelve-foot-high fence, which sentries regularly walked. Because Elmira was so deep into Union territory, and the prison populace generally was in such poor physical condition, serious escape attempts were few; there were but four principal incidents. But Benson was constantly scheming and ever on the alert for any opportunity. On the night of 6 October 1864, he and ten other men did at last successfully escape. It was multiply fortunate for them, because by that time conditions had deteriorated badly and the death rate was picking up alarmingly. Inside the prison the worst was still to come during the ensuing winter.

The historical novelist MacKinley Kantor wrote *Andersonville*, a Pulitzer Prize–winning account of the infamous Confederate prison in Georgia. He might well have written another about the awful place five miles north of the Pennsylvania boundary, which the southerners called "Helmira." Even one northern soldier suggested that "a cat, notwithstanding its proverbial nine lives, wouldn't last five months" inside Elmira. But Benson and his ten companions were spared the worst of times there. Some of the escapees went to Canada. Benson, however, made his way alone from western New York back to Robert E. Lee's army in Petersburg, Virginia, by any means necessary—including walking, hopping trains, riding stolen horses, and even swimming the Potomac.

On the way, Benson encountered Lieutenant Colonel John S. Mosby and his band of guerrilla soldiers. Mosby welcomed him and offered advice on how best to proceed—stick close to the mountains. Benson would have preferred to go on a raid with Mosby's men, for he was much impressed with them. "I am quite sure," he recalled, "that this band was of better calibre in all respects, physically and mentally, than the general run of soldiers." But no horse could be found for him.

By 27 October 1864, Benson had made his way to Brigadier General Bradley T. Johnson's brigade headquarters. Like Mosby, Johnson eagerly listened to Benson's amazing report of his adventures. "The Sergeant talks mighty well, don't he?" Benson—who thought himself not very eloquent—proudly recalled having heard Johnson say at the conclusion of his account.

Then Benson was sent to New Market, Virginia, to have an audience with the commander of the Second Corps, Army of Northern Virginia, Lieutenant General Jubal A. Early. That general arranged for the last leg of Benson's journey, via stagecoach to Staunton and train to Richmond and then to Lee's besieged army at Petersburg. "I am not dead, but alive and well. Just escaped from prison," Benson telegraphed his doubtlessly relieved family.

To write his memoir, thirteen years after the war had ended, Benson consulted diaries that he and his brother, Blackwood, had kept. They helped him immeasurably to prepare so accurate a written recollection, for as he admitted "many incidents . . . have passed entirely out of my memory." But some of the wartime events he would never forget, and *they*, he asserted, "stand out as fresh and distinct as if they happened thirteen days ago instead of now thirteen years."

Aged twenty-two at the war's end, Benson lived well into his eightieth year. Moderately successful financially as a public accountant, he had a happy life as a family man, was active in Confederate veteran organizations, and did much writing— some of it of an historical nature, but mostly in the realm of philosophical opinion.

Here now is a good story about the Civil War—a very well told one, by a keenly interesting young enlisted participant in the conflict. Here's a confident prediction that you will enjoy it as much as have I.

Herman Hattaway
1992

☆　　☆

Preface

BERRY Greenwood Benson was born February 9, 1843, in Hamburg, South Carolina, just across the Savannah River from Augusta, Georgia, the oldest child of Abraham and Nancy Harmon Benson. He attended Mr. Griffin's school in Augusta until he was seventeen and a half years old, at which time his father took him into a firm of cotton factors as assistant bookkeeper. But he was not to remain there long; before he was eighteen he had joined one of the companies of Minute Men being formed throughout South Carolina, his brother Blackwood, not yet sixteen, joining at the same time.

On January 8, 1861, his company was mustered into service at Charleston, South Carolina. Thus Berry and Blackwood served in the Army of the Confederacy from the first shot at Sumter to the last at Appomattox, absent only when invalided home to recover from wounds, and in Berry's case during five months in Yankee prisons. They served in Jackson's "footcavalry" until their beloved general's death, and later in the Battalion of Sharpshooters attached to Gen. Maxcy Gregg's 1st South Carolina Volunteers, which became General McGowan's Brigade after General Gregg was killed. Both brothers were soon non-commissioned officers, and before the war was over Berry was several times in command of his company.

While holding a high score as a marksman, Berry was soon singled out for scouting, a work which he loved, and for which he was peculiarly fitted. It was on an expedition behind the enemy lines to get information wanted by General

Lee that he was captured and confined in Point Lookout Prison, where he remained only two days before making his escape and setting out to re-join Lee's army. He got back into Virginia by swimming the Potomac below Washington, but was re-captured near Washington, and confined first in the Old Capitol Prison, then sent to Elmira, New York. Searching around immediately for possibilities of escape, he soon became a ringleader in the group of ten men who made the only successful tunnel escape in Elmira's history—though a number of other tunnels were started.

Making his way back through three states, Berry rejoined the Sharpshooters in defense of Petersburg, and was in the battered remnants of Lee's Army in the final retreat to Appomattox. But neither Berry nor Blackwood would accept defeat. Learning of the impending surrender, they told a few friends, including General McGowan, that they were going to join General Johnston in North Carolina. Then they stole through the enemy pickets, and set off for North Carolina, where they found General Johnston on the point of surrender. So, still bearing the rifles which to this day have never been surrendered, the boys headed for their home in Augusta, Georgia.

After the war, Berry taught school for a while, later becoming a public accountant. Always good at mathematics, he invented an improved system of bookkeeping, which became widely used until it was supplanted by machines. On February 6, 1868, he married Jeanie Oliver of Augusta, daughter of Major Stephen Oliver, C.S.A. To them were born two sons and four daughters.

During the war, Berry and Blackwood both kept diaries, but when Berry was captured the section which he had in his pocket was taken from him. Thirteen years after the war, Berry assembled what was left of his own diary, borrowed the part of Blackwood's covering the missing section of his own, and, further aided by letters carefully preserved by the family, wrote these reminiscences, intended as a record for his descendants. With this object in view, he included much that was primarily of family interest, the narrative sometimes following a wandering course, as one thing suggested another.

My editorial task has been mainly one of eliminating material not directly concerned with his war experiences. Except for some necessary transitions and summaries to cover omissions, I am proud to have Berry Benson tell his own story in his own words.

In addition to his memoirs, Berry Benson wrote many articles for newspapers, and he contributed a chapter to a history of Elmira Prison. He also wrote on philosophical subjects for the old *Outlook* and for *Century Magazine*. It turned out that Blackwood also developed a flair for writing. He published three historical novels on the Civil War before settling down to a successful business career first in Atlanta, then in Austin, Texas.

When a Confederate monument was erected in Augusta, Berry Benson's figure was chosen to go on top, where it now overlooks Broad Street. He died on January 1, 1923. Some years later, his son Charles Greenwood Benson placed the original hand-written manuscript of the memoirs in the Southern Historical Collection of the University of North Carolina Library.

Athens, Georgia   SUSAN WILLIAMS BENSON

☆ 1 ☆

A Young Volunteer

THE FIRST SIX MONTHS — BATTLE OF COLD HARBOR
— THE REMAINING SEVEN DAYS

☆ ☆ ☆ ☆ ☆ ☆ ☆ ☆ ☆ ☆ ☆

ALREADY in the fall of 1860, companies of Minute Men were being formed throughout S. C. holding themselves in readiness to be under arms at a minute's notice. One being formed in Hamburg, Blackwood and I joined it, and its services were proffered to the Governor. On the 8th of Jany. 1861, nineteen days after S. C. seceded, our Co. with two others from Edgefield District, by command of the Govr. took train at Hamburg, to be mustered into service at Charleston, I lacking one month of being 18 years of age, and Blackwood four months of being 16. We left in a storm of cheers, Father giving us a little money, a little good advice, and his blessing.

On our arrival at Charleston that evening we were quartered in a steamboat (the "Excel") lying at the wharf, and next day were marched to the Arsenal and furnished with arms, smoothbore muskets, carrying a ball and three buckshot for cartridge. The distribution was made in an upper story, and the men were cautioned about a large square opening in the floor (through which goods were pulled up, I suppose). But notwithstanding the caution, one man (Sidney Weeks of Merriwether Guards) unfortunately fell through, and striking his head on the brick pavement below, was killed, probably the first life lost in the war.

We were now boated over to Sullivan's Island, and mustered into the state's service for six months. There were some

1

other companies already arrived and perhaps others came just after; the 1st. Regt. S. C. Volunteers was formed, under Col. Maxcy Gregg. We entered at once upon a soldier's duty, drilling, mounting guard, picket duty etc. The island is almost pure sand, the vegetation being palmetto trees and myrtle bushes. There was nothing along the beach to break the force of the wind, and some of the coldest night-watches I ever spent was along the shore.

Shortly after, the Regt. was transferred to Morris Island, landing at Cumming's Point, soon to be famous as the locale of the yet unbuilt Iron Battery. I did not stay long with the Regt. A one-gun battery was about to be built not far above Cumming's Point, to be in command of Col. Tom Lamar of Edgefield Dist. and I was one of eight taken from the Regt. to man it. And now we worked hard, often by night as well as by day, shoveling sand and rolling wheelbarrows of sand up plank inclines, and many a time we were wet through by rain, not being allowed to stop. Once having no dry garment to sleep in, I took a cotton sack and cutting a hole in the bottom for my head, and a hole in each side for my arms, I had a sleeveless shirt. Taking another sack, I cut two holes in the bottom, thrust my legs through, and tying the mouth of the sack about my waist, I had a pair of drawers. These sacks were used to fill with sand, and were then piled up like bricks to make a wall.

One of our number (Burdell) was relieved from work to cook. Our rations were very liberal, being the U. S. Regulation rations of the time. Besides, we were helped out with oysters—the small raccoon oyster which grew in large beds all about—and crabs. I was No. 5 at the gun—the one who pulled the trigger. Just to the right of us, as we faced the sea, was the battery of the Charleston Artillery, and farther on the Star-of-the-West and the Dahlgren batteries. To our left was the biggest battery of all, the Trapier Battery, and the mortar Battery; and down at the point the Iron Battery, which fronted Ft. Sumter, its upper surface being covered by a roof-work of iron rails from a railroad, the roof being inclined toward the fort, so that a shot from the fort would rebound from it. . . . This was the child-parent of the now teeming race of ironclads and monitors. . . .

One day, lying down in the tent, thinking of nothing in particular (not counting my sweetheart), I was startled by a heavy boom up the island. Up and out to the gun! But before we could reach it, another report, and another! An eye cast to sea, and a sail vessel skimming along with the wind, the stars and stripes afloat at her masthead. A quick trailing of the gun, a hasty sight, a jerk at the lanyard, and I had fired my first hostile shot—64 pounds of solid iron. Then down came the flag, hauled down by frightened hands, till it dipped in the water at the side. A boat was sent out to her, and she proved to be a schooner loaded with ice for Charleston. She had been a long time out, from Maine, and her master knew nothing of the troubles in Charleston Harbor.

Before the winter was over there was some very cold weather, the winds came blowing down the beach, keen and sharp, carrying sand with it which one was lucky not to have blown into his eyes. Once we had quite a snow. On Sullivan's Island our water was got from the great cistern under the Moultrie House, which had a plentiful supply, but on Morris Island we had to dig holes in the sand, which soon became partly filled with clear water sometimes of good taste, but usually more or less brackish. These we called springs, and they rose and fell with the tide. A spring that might be fresh at the first making was apt to become salty after a little using. This lack of sweet water and the attacks of the sand flies as spring came on, were our greatest troubles.

On the 12th of April 1861, at earliest dawn, a shot at Fort Johnson on James' Island sounded the opening of the war. We took our posts by our gun, which pointed seaward to fire upon the vessels should they attempt to come in. We watched the curving lines of fire as shells streamed from the encircling forts upon Sumter. The attack was received a long time in silence; but at length the reply came, and many a shot was rained upon the iron battery, which afterward showed heavy scars. The balls rebounded from the iron surface, and fell into the marsh beyond, or into one of the channels winding through it. One shot came bounding and skipping along toward us, and rolled right past our battery. Upon this Col. Lamar (who had been ordered not to fire upon the Fort, but was longing to do it) made this an excuse and trained the gun around. Upon the word Fire, No. 5 (myself) pulled his lanyard, and an unauthorized 64 lb. shot sailed away into the fort.

The bombardment continued all that day and into the night—I believe, all night. Next day the barracks were fired by hot shot, and the Fort presented a grand spectacle with its vast column of smoke floating away, through which the flag could now and then be caught sight of, while her guns plied sullen work. Sometime in the forenoon the flagstaff was shot away. Seeing the flag disappear, we thought it meant surrender, but directly it went up again on a shorter improvised staff.

Toward noon the fort surrendered, Anderson and his men being allowed to march out with the honors of war. Next day, Sunday, the Steamer Isabel stood up to the Fort, and took them out to the U. S. fleet on the bar.

A short time after the fall of Fort Sumter, the Regt. was given the option of going home or going to Virginia to finish out our six months' service. Many went home & amongst them many officers, the result of which was the breaking up of some companies. Our officers all going home, Blackwood and I joined a Fairfield Dist. Co.—"I", under Capt. John Davis.

Va. had seceded, but N. C. had not, so we had to pass through U. S. territory. Our trip was an ovation, cheers, bonfires, speeches, etc. At Richmond, we were quartered in the Old Fair Grounds, where our dress parades were attended by large crowds of ladies & men every evening. When we walked through the streets we were objects of universal attention, and if we wanted to buy anything at a store, the chances were we would be forbidden to pay for it. On one occasion, I bought a pair of shoes, and the seller refused to take the money. When he saw I was determined to pay, he took it, and picking up a small cheese fairly forced it upon me. . . . But how all that changed in fair Richmond! Soon the soldier was of less esteem than the civilian, begging such few favors as he received, not having them forced upon him. The change was but natural, for where one may entertain two, he may not entertain a thousand. . . .

[EDITOR'S NOTE: On May 23rd the regiment left Richmond by train for Manassas Junction, where it camped, doing some picket duty at Bull Run. On June 16th, 1862, they started marching towards the Potomac. But after reaching the railroad at Vienna, firing upon a train, and burning seven cars, they were moved back to Germantown, Virginia.]

I had hoped extremely on our late expedition, that we would reach the Potomac. The feeling so continued to work upon me that I finally felt as though I *must* see the river, and so on Saturday June 23rd I started to the Potomac alone. Going over the ground we had recently marched over, I finally got off the track. In the evening, somewhere near Drainsville I fell in with some Confed. Black Horse Cavalry, who arrested me. I was sent back on a horse, under guard, to camp, and was placed under arrest. How long I stayed in the guard house I don't remember, only I know I wrote a letter to the Col. trying to explain my ambition to view the rolling flood of the Potomac & praying for deliverance. No attention being paid to which, I looked about to effect my own deliverance. The chance soon offered. The guard house was an ordinary A tent, and the guard posted over it would let me sit outside the door when I liked. I was sitting outside the tent thus, talking with the guard, when another came up to relieve him.

"What have I got to guard?" asked the newcomer.

This and this and this, said the old one, naming sundry articles of camp equipage, but omitting to include the prisoner.

No sooner was the old guard out of sight than I got up and walked away too. When the order came for my release, I was some miles away from camp on some other expedition, and found upon my return that there was some surprise at my second absence. But I got no punishment for it. I suppose they deemed me incorrigible as to my rambling propensities.

On 2nd July, we started home, the six months' service being fulfilled, none of us having any presentiment of the great battle that would so soon (July 21) be fought on the very ground we were quitting. We were coming back so soon; a battle would hardly be fought in that little while.

We reached home July 12; and on Sunday we went to church in Augusta, where I noticed a wonderful thinning out amongst the men. War had already taken so many away.

Before leaving Richmond, Brother and I had promised Wm. T. Haskell, a member of the Regt., to join a company he was making up. So on July 31, we went to Charleston & met Haskell, & proceeded thence with others of the Co. to Richmond, which we reached 4 Aug. We were camped first in Old Fair Ground, then in New Fair Ground, then at the Rocketts.

The Regt. was now sent to Suffolk, where the organization was completed. There were 11 companies: 10 infantry, 1 artillery. The artillery Co. under McIntosh did not stay with us long but was ordered to its proper place with other artillery. We pitched tents on a plain, and went through the usual duties of roll call, drills, etc. Our captain was Wm. T. Haskell of Abbeville; 1st Lieut. Jno. G. Barnwell of Beaufort; 2nd Lieut. Grimke Rhett of Beaufort; 3rd Lieut. Wm. Hutson Wigg. But on the latter's resignation shortly after, his place was filled by Charles Pinckney Seabrook of Beaufort. The men were from many quarters, Charleston and Beaufort mostly, perhaps, but also from Abbeville, Edgefield, Savannah & elsewhere. I think the Capt. tried to get up a select Co. We had some excellent material. Our 1st Sergt., Frank Frost, was early detached and appointed Asst. Surgeon, then Surgeon, then Brigade Surgeon, then Asst. Corps Surgeon.

Capt. Haskell was not, strictly speaking, a martinet, but he was the strictest officer in the regiment (except it might be Lt. Rhett) and the whole Regt. was soon hating him and Rhett cordially. But after a time, they not diminishing their discipline, all the men came to see that this discipline was best for all concerned, and at last they were esteemed as highly as they had been hated deeply. They soon had Co. H. so prompt and proficient in all duties & so well drilled that the Col. once spoke of us as a model company. This the others took up and for a long time after, in jealousy, used to speak of us derisively as "The Models." But we noticed that the other officers began to "model" their companies also.

As winter drew near, the whole Regiment was put to work, building substantial quarters of pine logs chinked with mud. Each company built its own, which consisted of one long house, divided by partitions into rooms for the different messes. The houses were arranged in order with a street about 30 ft. wide between them, and at the end of the street was built a small house for the officers of the Co. whose quarters fronted the street. The companies were divided into messes, about 8 men each, with a non-commissioned officer in charge of each mess. Having been made a Corporal, I had charge of a mess, whose names were as below, as I take them from my diary. In forming messes, there was nothing like compulsion, the men drifting together as their own social desires prompted. It may be the non-com officer wasn't always as well pleased as he might be, but none ever tore his hair. Here is the list:

Berry G. Benson	Hamburg, S. C.
James Larkin	Charleston, S. C.
	(native of Baltimore)
John C. Calhoun Veitch	Charleston, S. C.
Albert P. Youmans	Beaufort, S. C.
James E. Bail	Charleston, S. C.
B. K. Benson	Hamburg, S. C.
Charles H. Munnerlyn	Orangeburg, S. C.
E. M. Box	Beaufort, S. C.

A short history of the fate of each may not be out of place. *Larkin*, a sail maker, escaped unwounded, I believe, until leading a charge at Gettysburg, while carrying the regimental colors (a large heavy blue silk flag with a palmetto tree worked on one side, a present from the ladies of S. C. to the old 1st) he was shot through the right breast, and after the retreat fell into the enemy's hands. They treated him very kindly. Indeed his wound was so severe that, had he not been captured, he would probably have died in a Confed. hospital. For we had not the means and appliances the enemy had. He was exchanged & subsequently rejoined us, but did not stay long, being subject to hemorrhages, the result of his wound. I think he attained the rank of Lieut.

Veitch, on June 27/62 was mortally wounded in the battle of Cold Harbor. He was next man on my right when shot. He died July 6, at S. C. hospital in Manchester.

Albert Youmans survived the war, a good soldier. I don't remember his being wounded except once—battle of the Wilderness.

Bail, a printer, came out with Larkin (two chums), slept with Blackwood and me the night of Aug. 28/62. Next day, battle of 2nd Manassas, he was shot dead by a bullet through the head. On 30th Larkin and I buried him in his blanket on the field where he fell.

Munnerlyn, an overseer, was the butt of the mess. All kinds of jokes were launched at him. Sanguine temperament, with florid face and red hair, he was easily moved to wrath, but quickly recovered his good humor, for he could not hold malice. Of a multitude of nicknames bestowed upon him, the one which clung was "old Son." He was wounded slightly at 2nd Manassas.

Box (like Veitch) was killed in his first battle, being shot dead (a bullet through the head, I believe) at Cold Harbor or Manassas, June 27, 1862.

Of the eight men in our mess therefore, three were killed in battle, and the other five were all wounded in one battle or another. The history of our mess would be a fair measure of the fortunes of other companies and regiments throughout the army. Towards the end of the war, it was rare to see a soldier who had not at some time received a wound. It is no wonder Grant found it hard to crush Lee. The enemy he was fighting were all veterans.

[EDITOR'S NOTE: From winter quarters in Suffolk, the brigade was transferred first to Goldsboro, North Carolina, then by rail to Fredericksburg. In May 1862 they fell back on Richmond, making the march of sixty miles "heavily encumbered with arms, ammunition, and other impedimenta. We had not yet learned how to save muscle by throwing away property." June 25, 1862, began the march up the Chickahominy. On the afternoon of the 26th, they crossed the river, and shortly after, heard firing in front. This was the Battle of Mechanicsville. They were drawn up in line and ordered to lie down, being held in support. Bullets began to drop among them and a few were wounded. But the sun soon set and they were not called into action.

Next day, June 27th, they advanced, and towards noon caught up with the enemy, who had just vacated a camp and taken position on the brow of a steep hill across a stream].

Co. H. under Capt. Haskell was in advance of the Regt., deployed as skirmishers. As soon as we came in sight, being in their deserted camp, the enemy opened fire on us from the hill opposite. We returned the fire, quickly taking shelter behind boxes, barrels, or whatever lay about. But before I had reached a cluster of empty barrels, I felt a bullet strike my right foot. Looking down, I saw a dent in the edge of my shoe sole, near my big toe.

I had fired only once or twice from behind the barrels when Veitch, across the camp street, suddenly called, "Benson, I am shot." I ran to him, and found that a bullet had struck him in the breast. Two of us carried him into a tent close by, doing what we could for him in the few minutes we could snatch from the fight, and I received his last message to his sister, "Give her my love, and tell her I died for my country."

Our line pressed forward, going down the hill in a run and across the stream and charging up the hill, which we took. Here we paused to rest. . . . We again took up the pursuit and found the enemy waiting for us in a belt of pine woods whence they had command of our approach through an open field. We pressed on despite their fire, broke into a charge and cleared the woods, whence we saw their scattered ranks fleeing through the fields.

Later in the day we drew up at the foot of a gentle decline, our line running along a small stream we had just crossed. We were ordered to lie down. And this was necessary if no immediate advance were planned, for bullets and shells came hot and fast, with a terrible din of battle raging in front and on the right. What we had seen before was child's play. Men were killed and wounded amongst us everywhere. As I lay, a man on my right suddenly vomited blood and turned over and died. Wounded men kept rising and running to the rear. A bullet struck me on my right shoulder, making only a severe bruise. A shell struck beside me and threw mud all over me, filling one ear. Lieut Rhett was killed. Box of my mess was killed. Many were wounded.

Then came the order to fall back. Demoralization ensued; the Regt. became scattered. I looked for my brother but could not find him. I saw Capt. Haskell, a few men with him, slowly giving way to the rear, and I joined them. Then came a fresh line advancing. We joined them and crossed the stream again, into the fields beyond.

Then I saw a glorious sight—A regiment (30th N. C.) with Capt. Thomas M. Blount, Quartermaster of 4th N. C. at the head on horseback with the battle flag in his hand, the men following at a run, waving their hats and cheering—charging for the top of the hill. I shall never see such a sight again, as long as I live. And all the while, the din and roar, the pulse of artillery, the cheers and cries of "Forward! Forward!" and the gray smoke mixed with it all! This was the battle of Cold Harbor, and never since, unless at Spottsylvania, have I heard such a roar of musketry. For hours, absolutely unbroken by a pause, it was like the steady falling of water.

Again I became separated from the men I knew; I found myself in a charge with a line of N. C. troops. I gained the front. The charge was at its height, when there came a slackening, a hesitation, a pause, and back went the line in confusion, when half a minute more should have carried the crest. As we fled, the bullets seemed to come thicker. Cries of "Rally!" sounded on all sides, but there was no rally under such a fire. In this rout, I met up with Larkin of my company and my mess. We crept slowly to the rear, completely worn out, and threw ourselves on the ground. Hampton's Legion passed by, and a few minutes after we heard their cheers, having I believe, carried the hill.

It was now growing dark, and the battle ceased except for sputterings here and there. Instead of the rattle of guns, I now heard on all sides groans, and cries from the wounded of "water! water!" We gave till our canteens were empty. Till late into the night men were calling for their regiments, endeavoring to collect together, for the confusion and commingling had been very great. Calling so for 1st S. C., Larkin and I received an answer from one of our company named Rice, who told me my brother was wounded. He led us to where Blackwood lay, with a wound through the left thigh. Not knowing where the command (or any part of it) was, we four lay together till morning, a dead man at our feet, and dead men all about us.

When day came we made a stretcher of a blanket and two poles cut from the woods, and carried Blackwood to the Field Hospital, which was a large farmhouse, where his wound was pronounced a flesh wound only. Then the three of us returned to seek the Regt. Before leaving the hospital, I went in the garden and was shocked to see lying about it, hands and arms and legs that had been amputated—a dreadful sight. We found a portion of the Regt.—it had not all got together yet—and Lt. Col. Hamilton made us a speech saying, "One more glorious day like yesterday and our country is free!"

Whilst the regiment rested here, I walked up to a little house near by, where lay the body of our Lieut. Grimke Rhett. With a pair of scissors that lay on the mantelshelf, I cut a lock of hair from his head and put it in my note book. All of it has since been lost except one single strand, which I fix here. I also picked up on the field a bloody leaf, and placed it in my book. The leaf has been lost, but its imprint is left on the page, showing the dark stain of blood. Thus closed the two days of Mechanicsville and Cold Harbor, we being only under fire in the former, but in the thick of the latter.

In this battle knapsacks were captured by thousands, while the whole Confed. army refitted itself with blankets, rubber clothes, tent flies, haversacks and canteens. So that in the middle of the war and later, to see equipment of Southern make was somewhat of a curiosity.

During the rest of the Seven Days' Battle we were continually on the march, sometimes under fire, but we never had such a set-to as on 27th. At Malvern Hill we were not called into action, but we passed over the field just afterward, and a bloody one it was for the Confederates. . . .

The chase after the enemy was a hot one. Midsummer, the weather was very warm, and the continual stirring of the dust on the roads rendered the air almost unbreathable. Nose, eyes, mouth, ears, hair, and clothes became filled with dust, which even found its way into the throat and had to be spit out. Not only the fences and grass, but even the houses and trees became covered with a coating of this dust, so that the woods bordering the roads showed a dull dead grey instead of living green.

One day as we passed a large house with a lawn in front, there at the gate stood a negro nurse with a pretty baby in her arms. As the long column of rough, ragged, dirty, battle-worn soldiers filed by, every eye was turned to the child, and all were saying, one to another, "Look at the baby!" And many a ragged sleeve that was raised to the face under cover of wiping away dust came away with a wet spot upon it, doubt not. Long after when we were in the Valley on the march one day I said something about the incident. Lieut. Miller spoke up, smiling, "Why, do you remember that baby? I thought everybody but me had forgotten it." Miller fell at Petersburg, and now perhaps I am the only one that remembers the baby.

The weather was very hot and the march so exhausting that many fell with sunstroke, and many more became utterly used up for the time. Whenever we crossed a stream tin cups were brought into requisition. Canteens were hastily filled, a long cool draught taken, and a full cup handed to the man behind you with the request, "Pour this down my back." And on we plodded, wet to the knees or thighs it might be, but feeling wonderfully revived.

Once on this march, as we were hurrying on, passing here and there those who, fagged out, had lain down at the side of the road to rest, I suddenly saw thrust out an arm holding a tin cup. A pleading voice came from the wan, weary face of a boy who sat leaning against a tree. What stone-hearted devil possessed me to pass that sick boy, not stopping to drain my canteen into his cup, I cannot tell. I think I trusted to someone more kind hearted than me stopping to relieve him. All soldiers know what exertion and fatigue are entailed to regain one's place in a hurried march, when one has dropped out for ever so short a time. But fatigue and discomfort would have been a small price to pay, to buy away the voice that has so often since sounded in my ears, "Please give me a sup in my tin."

Having pursued the enemy as far as we could, we camped and rations were issued, meat and flour. If I remember rightly, these were the first rations issued to us since the march began. We had been living on the spoils from the enemy. But now not a cooking utensil of any kind could be had. . . . Some heated stones, some baked in the ashes. I cast about and found an old broken plough-share in a field on which we baked. But the neatest device of all was the making of the dough into a long rope, which was then wrapped spirally around a ram-rod, the ramrod then being laid horizontally before the fire on two small wooden forks set in the ground. By turning the ramrod, all parts of the dough were by turns exposed to the fire and so baked, being broken off in pieces when done.

We now marched back through the battlefields, to camp at Laurel Hill Church, near Richmond. On this march, and on the latter ones of the fighting, we endured at times almost agony from the horrible stench that in one locality or another pervaded the air. I suppose these odors arose principally from dead horses, as probably all, or nearly all, the men were buried. But it must be confessed that burial was too often so shallow that it would be no wonder if the little earth that covered the bodies proved a feeble disinfectant. How oppressive and penetrating such odors may be, can be imagined from the citation of one instance; in passing a dead horse on the road I hoped to escape by doubling up my blanket and breathing through the folds. But it did little good; the horrible scent still penetrated; having passed by I counted the folds and there were seven, I being nearly suffocated from the difficulty in getting air at all through so much obstruction.

During the latter part of this campaign, I marched barefoot, having discarded my worn shoes for a pair from a knapsack I picked up near where I slept one night. But the exchange was no profit, for soon these came so much to pieces that I threw them away. Fortunately I am tough-footed and it was summer.

Have you ever seen a proud man? One who looked proud? I have seen the personification of pride; a man bearing in his face the proudest look I ever saw in mortal man. And he was barefoot. It was in the Valley, after the battle of Sharpsburg, as we were marching along the turnpike, a new fallen snow on the ground, that, happening to cast my eyes to one side, I saw him, a young man, tall and vigorous, but utterly barefoot in the snow, standing in a fence corner, his gun leaning against his shoulder, and of all proud faces I have ever seen, his was the proudest. It was a pride that seemed to scorn not only the privation and cold, but the exposure of his sufferings to other eyes, and even the very pity that it called forth.

Whilst camped at Laurel Hill Church, I made a visit to my brother, who was progressing very favorably with his wound, at Byrd Island hospital in Richmond.

Shortly after, we were ordered to get ready to march. I don't know how I came to do the cooking for our mess this time, for it was a duty I shunned whenever possible. However it was, I set to work, and there being plenty of flour and bacon set out in the Co. street to help myself to, I cooked 96 biscuits, besides some thin wafers without salt. These latter were an experiment which didn't meet with the success anticipated, for the others of the mess rejected them to a man. To prove that it was the fault of their own depraved tastes, I ate the last one of them—and was glad when I had done so. I never made any more.

This move was to join Stonewall Jackson at Gordonsville, under whom we remained thereafter till his death.

2

Under Stonewall Jackson

JACKSON'S FOOTCAVALRY — MANASSAS JUNCTION — ILL AND A STRAGGLER — SHARPSBURG AND BOTELER'S FORD — FREDERICKS-BURG — WINTER QUARTERS, 1862-63 — STONEWALL JACKSON

☆ ☆ ☆ ☆ ☆ ☆ ☆ ☆ ☆ ☆ ☆

SHORTLY after being put under Jackson, we began to march. The movement culminated in the attack on Pope at Cedar Mountain, Aug. 9, 1862. In this battle our brigade had no active part, being held as rear guard for the protection of the army train, though our brigadier, Gen. Gregg, chafed very much at thus being kept out of the battle.

The night before the battle, not knowing that we would not be engaged next day; indeed, taking it for granted we would be, there were many little private talks around the fires, friends giving instructions to do so and so in case of being killed, to write to such and such a one, and say —

Sergt. Mackey gave a number of messages to the men to take to his people at home, saying he felt that he was to be killed next day. On the eve of all our battles there was of course more or less of this forethought and preparation for death, but I remember it particularly of this one. Due, it may be, to the strain of my own thoughts at the time;—just as probably like action on my own part on the eve of the battle of Chancellorsville causes me to remember especially vividly, the number of men I then saw looking into their bibles, picking out here and there favorite texts for comfort and encouragement. And it was with no degree whatever of shamefacedness that the men, at such solemn times, turned

16

to their Testaments; and the book would, not unlikely, be passed from one to another. And such men were foremost in the charge and rearmost in retreat.

After this fight with Pope we had hardly time to collect our thoughts before we were again in motion. And now (Aug. 16) began Jackson's famous flank march which culminated in the battle of 2nd Manassas, and the invasion of Maryland. Having been moved here and there, shifting positions, we camped one night in the woods. Next morning early, Aug. 25th, we obeyed the usual order to fall in, getting under arms and into line. Then came the unexpected command, "Unsling knapsacks." With doubtful faces, as though maybe we had not heard right, we unslung our knapsacks and laid them on the ground. "Left face! Forward march!" And from that day to this not one of us has seen his knapsack again.

Swiftly along the high country roads, day long and far into the night, through the fields to make short cuts, letting down bars here, or pulling down a panel of fence there to pass through, along byways and farm roads—always the bee line—we pushed. Unencumbered by wagons, glad to rest and sleep when the night's halt was made, no rations issued, faring on green corn and apples from the fields, helped out by such bread and butter and milk as we had money to buy from the people, or they would give, so Jackson's "foot cavalry" went hurrying northward to make a stand behind the enemy we had just fronted.

Even before the march had begun, I was taken sick, but not enough to go to the hospital. I continued on the march, often having to fall out of ranks and lie down to rest, catching up afterwards as best I could. There was excitement in the swift motion and pleasure in hailing friendly strangers. Jests were in constant play, and often some burst of song.

The turnpike had been passed over back and forth already during the war, by first one army and then the other. Although we were constantly greeted by the cry, "Hurrah for South Carolina!" there was with us a faint doubt whether the enemy might not receive from some of the people the same kind greeting—not from inclination, we knew well enough, but to keep on the good side of the powers that be. Well, in a little place called Harrisonville, we passed a house where some ladies were standing. As the head of the regiment came up, they asked, "What Regt. is this?"

"First South Carolina."

"Hurrah for South Carolina!" came the sweet voices of the dear women, chorussed at the close by the piping voice of a little fellow not much more than a baby, "Hurrah for Sout' Ca'liny Massachute!"

"Hush! Hush!" from the women, but the cat was out of the bag, and such a laugh as the boys set up! "Hurrah for Sout' Ca'liny Massachute" was a standing joke for a long time.

But it was only thought of as a good joke, for the people everywhere were eminently and truly patriotic, and they were exceedingly generous, and the women seemed to us very angels out of the sky. It was somewhere about Salem, I think, that two young women ran out from a house and stood at the gate, with eyes filled with tears, blessing us and telling us that though they had seen enemy soldiers in plenty, we were the first Confederate soldiers they had yet seen.

While marching through a village (I think it was Salem) I was greatly surprised and rejoiced to see Blackwood step out from a little knot of soldiers waiting at a corner, and take his place in the ranks by my side. I had supposed that he was at that moment in bed in the hospital at Richmond.

Sometimes passing one of those large Virginia mansions, or going through a village, we would find a group of ladies standing at the side of the road with buckets of milk or water, and maybe biscuits with ham or butter or cold chicken, which they would give over into the hands that would be thrust out to receive as the column of half famished men swept onward. Gratitude for such kindness we all felt of course, but gratitude didn't check the galling fire of banter which greeted any citizen man who showed himself within tongue-reach.

When a halt was made to sleep, all the houses in the neighborhood would be besieged by soldiers buying or begging something to eat. The earliest comers fared best, for they got the cooked provisions, while late comers must be content with flour, meal, and meat which they must cook themselves as best they could. Some of the men begged without any lack of cheek. One standard tale was of the fellow who appealed to the lady of the house: "Please ma'am, give me a drink of water, I'm so hungry, I ain't got no place to sleep."

I remember one day, just before reaching Manassas, we fared particularly ill for food. If I remember rightly, my only food that day was a handful of parched corn and three or four small, green, sour apples. On a forced march like this when the men are obliged to find food for themselves the best way they can, some men must of course fare much worse than others. At a time when a man as strong and active as myself could only provide himself with a handful of corn and a few hard, pinched apples, I think it not altogether unlikely that some men, as was told, were reduced to the extremity of picking grains of corn out of the horses' dung, washing it, and parching it for food. Think of the pluck that men must have, to endure such privation, and still unflinchingly keep their place in ranks, afraid to drop out lest they miss a battle!

I do not mean this praise of our own men as disparagement of the other side. On the contrary, I believe that they would have undergone as much, and doubtless in one form or another, often did.

From Salem we pushed on through Thoroughfare Gap to the east side of the Blue Ridge, and struck Manassas Junction, easily scattering the small force there and capturing untold army supplies, which, with ten locomotives and seven trains of cars, we burned, after taking for our own use whatever we wanted. It would be impossible to tell the variety of provisions and other goods we found here. I remember that one article in our dinner was fish, and that we had sugar and coffee, and there my memory fails me.

Having once broken up camp in winter quarters, the original messes had gradually dissolved and new ones formed, the men associating together as tastes and dispositions prompted. On the night before Manassas Junction, having halted in an open field somewhere near morning, my messmate, Bail, my brother and I had slept on the bare ground, without cover, huddled together to keep warm. So we slept this night at Manassas Junction, but now we had blankets, and the whole field was lit up by burning cars. Shells and ammunition boxes were bursting in the flames, the pieces every now and then dropping amongst the sleeping men. But the chance of getting hit kept nobody awake.

From Manassas Junction, having destroyed it, we marched northward to Centerville, thence back across Bull Run, crossing at or near Stone Bridge. Next day, Co. H. was thrown out on the flank of the moving column, indicating proximity to the enemy. And it was not long before we felt them. In a heavy wood open of undergrowth, the battle began. The line drew up in the wood, its left resting on an open field, a deep railroad cut in front. Co. H. was thrown across deployed as skirmishers, and advanced cautiously. We soon became engaged, fighting Indian fashion from behind trees. The enemy being in force and pressing us, the skirmish line drew back slowly upon the line of battle, taking our proper position on the left.

In a few minutes the roll of musketry became general and continuous along the line. Jackson was being assailed in heavy force. In our front, as soon as the battle opened, the enemy charged upon us, rushing up to the edge of the cut, the passage of which we disputed stubbornly. Driven back, they would again return to the charge, being checked only by the cut. Nor could we always keep them from crossing. Sometimes the charge would be so vigorous as to force us back, and then we could see them already crossed over to pursue. But we would rally directly, charge in turn, and sweep them back, perhaps to scale the wall and fight upon their ground. At close quarters, never but a little strip of ground betwixt us,

all day the battle raged fierce and bloody, swaying back and
forth over a space that did not exceed 200 yards in width,
I think, to cover the whole action of the brigade that day.

Once we were running in retreat when just as I raised my
right foot from the ground a bullet struck me under the sole of
the foot. It hurt for some time, and left a deep dent in the
sole of the shoe. We were driven back temporarily more than
once, but I think we never ran more than a hundred yards,
if so much, before rallying and coming back in counter
charge. It was at one of these critical times, our line in confusion and going full tilt pursued by the enemy who had
crossed the cut when a Lieut. of Co. L. who happened to
be close by, called out, "Benson, for God's sake stop!" I
shouted to Blackwood who was only a few steps ahead. He
came running back and with him Jones of Co. H. They rang-
ed themselves by my side, fronting the enemy. The line, seeing us forming, hurried quickly back. The flag was in position,
the color bearers having rallied just as Co. H. began to rally.
A yell was raised and back we went, carrying the enemy
across the cut.

The charge over, the Lieut. came from his company to
shake hands with me, and we congratulated each other on
the success of the rally. Poor fellow! He went through the
day, but just at nightfall when the battle was over, a stray
shell from a distance fell in the Regiment, killing him instantly.

The enemy was finally driven from his position just before night, when a successful movement on our right enfiladed the R. R. cut, and the enemy fled. Fighting almost
constantly, our brigade that day successfully resisted five
charges made by three brigades of Hooker's division, and
held the ground at night. But it cost us dear. Of 30 men that
Co. H. carried into action, 18 were killed or wounded. The
proportion in Co. L. was still greater. The loss in the Regt.
was 150 out of 285 carried into action.

We slept that night where we had fought, the dead and
the living mingled together. And my friend Bail was amongst
the dead.

Next day, 30 Augt. 1862 we did not move far, but lay in an old field behind some piles of fence rails, doing some sharp-shooting but not being actually engaged, though listening to a fearful battle going on not far away, the main battle of Second Manassas.

Since I am writing this as an heirloom for Benson 1963 which I hope will go down amongst my descendants for a long time, and since amongst those there will be many who will go through life without ever experiencing the excitement of battle, and who, unless they imbibe very different ideas of these things from what I did in my boyhood, before I had seen for myself, may get quite false notions in regard to it, I want to try to tell something of how the fighting really goes on. I supposed a battle was carried on in the order and style of a first-class drill, knees all bent at the same angle and at the same moment, guns leveled on a line that was even as a floor, and every trigger pulled at one moment making a single report.

For a battlefield is not a drillroom, nor is battle an occasion for drill, and there is the merest semblance of order maintained. I say *semblance* of order, for there *is* an under-current of order in tried troops that surpasses that of the drillroom;—it is that order that springs from the confidence comrades have in each other, from the knowledge that these messmates of yours, whether they stand or lie upon the ground, close together or scattered apart, in front of you three paces, or in rear of you six, in the open or behind a tree or a rock, —that these, though they do not "touch elbows to the right," are nevertheless keeping dressed upon the colors in some rough fashion, and that the line will not move forward and leave them there, nor will they move back and leave the line.

A battle is entered into, mostly, in as good order and with as close a drill front as the nature of the ground will permit, but at the first "pop! pop!" of the rifles there comes a sudden loosening of the ranks, a freeing of selves from the impediment of contact, and every man goes to fighting on his own hook; firing as, and when he likes, and reloading as fast as he fires. He takes shelter wherever he can find it, so he does not get too far away from his Co., and his officers will call his attention to this should he move too far. He may stand up, he may kneel down, he may lie down, it is all right;— tho' mostly the men keep standing, except when silent under fire—then they lie down.

And it is not officers alone who give orders, the command to charge may come from a private in the line whose quick eye sees the opportunity, and whose order brooks then no delay. Springing forward, he shouts "charge, boys, charge!" The line catches his enthusiasm, answers with yells and follows him in the charge. Generally it is a wild and spontaneous cry from many throats along the line, readily evoked by the least sign of wavering in the enemy.

A battle is too busy a time, and too absorbing, to admit of a great deal of talk, still you will hear such remarks and questions as "How many cartridges you got?"—"My gun's getting mighty dirty."—"What's become of Jones?"—"Looky here, Butler, mind how you shoot; that ball didn't miss my head two inches." "Just keep cool, will you; I've got better sense than to shoot anybody." "Well, I don't like your standing so close behind me, nohow."—"I say, look at Lieut. Dyson behind that tree."—"Purty rough fight; ain't it Cap'n?"— "Cap'n, don't you think we better move up a little, just along that knoll?"—all this mixed and mingled with fearful yells, and maybe curses too, at the enemy.

And a charge looks just as disorderly. With a burst of yells, a long, wavering, loose jointed line sweeps rapidly forward, only now and then one or two stopping to fire, while here and there drop the killed and the wounded; the slightly wounded, some of them, giving no heed but rushing on, while others run hurriedly, half-bent, to the rear. The colors drop, are seized again,—again drop, and are again lifted, no man in reach daring to pass them by on the ground.—colors, not bright and whole and clean as when they came fresh from the white embroidering fingers, but since clutched in the storm of battle with grimy, bloody hands, and torn into shreds by shot and shell.

Oh, how it thrilled the heart of a soldier, when he had been long away from the army, to catch sight again of his red battle flag, upheld on its white staff of pine, its tatters snapping in the wind! A red rag, (there be those who will say),—a red rag tied to a stick, and that is all! And yet— that red rag, crossed with blue, with white stars sprinkled the cross within, tied to a slim, barked pine sapling, with leather thongs cut from a soldier's shoe, this rough red rag my soul loved with a lover's love.

Sept. 1st 1862, while the army was on the march, I was too ill to keep up. Eating no food, obliged to stop often to rest, I had fallen far behind my command when the rearguard of the army came up, and the officer in command ordered me to march on. I answered that it was not my inclination to straggle, and that if he could make me go on, he would be doing what I could not make myself do.

He stood a little while deliberating, then said, "Well, if you can't go on, I don't suppose we can make you," and moved on. So I was in rear of the whole army.

Suddenly I heard musketry. In that instant I felt new life shoot through my veins. I jumped to my feet and hurried forward, asking every one I caught up with which way Gregg's Brigade had gone. Coming upon a brigade standing in a field, I approached the comdg officer, and he courteously pointed out the way. Next I came to Col. Pegram of the Artillery. He also kindly gave me further directions. As I came to the foot of a low open hill, I found myself amongst the bullets which were now coming faster. Half way up the hill I found the regiment lying down under fire. Meanwhile it had begun to rain. I hurried forward, struck the regiment on the right, and then ran down the line and lay down on the left of Co. H. Capt. Haskell chided me for coming, but I told him I could not stay behind and hear the brigade fighting. Directly I felt something fall lightly over my body. My captain had arisen and thrown his oilcloth over me to shield me from the rain, taking the storm himself. . . . Kindness was only one of many good traits in his character. He was as cool and courageous as he was kind.

We lay in the rain, under fire for a while, but did not become engaged. The battle lasted but a little while, Jackson having merely assailed a column of Pope's army. This was the battle of Ox Hill or Chantilly.

We continued the march, moving toward Leesburg. I became more and more weak, marching out of ranks nearly all the time. Early in the morning, before the line could get started, I would go ahead in order not to be left too far behind at night. I was marching along by myself this way one morning when the head of the brigade came up behind me. In advance rode two officers, one of whom I saw to be Gen. Gregg. As they came up, I recognized in my brigadier's companion Gen. Jackson. As they rode up, he was speaking, and I heard him say, "There are but few commanders who appreciate the value of celerity." Those were his very words. It is the only time I ever heard him speak.

The day the army reached Leesburg (Sept 4) I was nearly played out, my Capt. begging me to stop and stay at some farm house till I got well. I answered no, that the army was going into Maryland, and that I was going too. I was out of ranks all day. Eating so little, I was very feeble. In the afternoon the last of the army passed me and I was left behind, creeping through Leesburg some time in the night. Some distance out of town, I found the Regt. asleep in a field. I stumbled on down to Co. H. and seeing two lying on a bed of wheat straw by a fire, I lay down on the edge of it without asking whose. It was Corp. Wigg and some other. Knowing I was ill, Wigg made room for me and spread the edge of his blanket over me. I never had the chance to repay him this little kindness. He was on the color-guard, and fell a few days after at Sharpsburg.

Next morning, Sept. 5, 1862, I fell in with the rest, but had to drop out before going twenty yards. I kept on slowly and saw the line come to a halt. I was glad to see them stop, for I saw plainly that there in full sight of the Maryland hills, I must leave the army, to have no share in its glory of invasion. No one may know with how heavy a heart I crept up to the captain to admit, "Captain, I can't go any farther."

He was glad I had made up my mind to stop, and gave me a note stating that I remained behind through illness, and requesting any good citizen to aid me. I could not bear to see the army move away from me, so I slowly crept away from it, aiming my course toward a large house about a mile off across the fields, stopping frequently to rest. Some time in the middle of the day I was about half way, feeling so exhausted that I thought I could never complete the journey. I stuck my ramrod in the ground with my handkerchief tied to the top, as a sign of distress. But no one came to my relief. Finally I crept on again, and just before sunset I lay down in the grass before the door, having been from sunrise to near sundown traveling one mile.

In a little while I was discovered and brought in and put to bed, and the family physician, Dr. Jackson, was sent to me. The owner of the place was a stately old gentleman, Judge Gray. It was due especially to the care given me by Miss Gray and a relative, Mrs. Grady, that my strength came back so rapidly. Having remained with these good people 5 days, I took my leave Sept. 10, despite their protests. Seeing me determined to go, they filled my haversack, begging me should fate ever bring me that way again to be sure to call on them. While I promised this, little did I dream that just two years after, I would be keeping that promise, glad to avail myself of it to get food and rest, and to hide from the enemy's cavalry that went to and fro through that country.

Gen. Lee had issued orders that all stragglers repair to Winchester, as to attempt to follow on after the army in Maryland would result in almost certain capture. So I headed west, crossed the Blue Ridge at Snicker's Gap, near Berryville, crossed the Shenandoah in a ferry boat, and went to Winchester. Determined not to enter the straggler's camp, I left Winchester going northward, leaving the main road to avoid the picket, and so on to Martinsburg. Before reaching Winchester there were a good many soldiers to be seen, stragglers, and scarcely ever but some were in sight on the roads.

Learning at Martinsburg that Jackson was about Harper's Ferry, I started thither. On the road, I heard citizens talking about volleys of artillery that rolled like musketry. I told them that necessarily they were mistaken, that it was musketry they had heard. No, they insisted, they had heard artillery roll like musketry. But I was still incredulous.

Just before reaching Harper's Ferry, I ran into a net. A soldier suddenly stepped out from a gateway and halted me. Though I expostulated, he said he must obey orders to stop all on the road and bring them into the stragglers' camp, to be distributed to their respective commands. Once in, I thought of nothing but how to get out. Sauntering down amongst the wagons parked close to the fence enclosing the grove, I watched my chance for a guard to turn his back, then I leaped the fence, ran through the high corn and got away. In an hour I was with "the boys," who declared themselves "powerful" glad to see me again, and gave me a full account of the battle of Harper's Ferry. I learned that our artillery, posted all around on the hills, had rained an unintermittent fire of shells upon the enemy's camp, forcing a prompt surrender. The capture was about 11,000 men with some 13,000 stand of arms, ammunition, provisions, and all kinds of army stores.

On 17th of Sept. 1862, began early in the morning the battle of Sharpsburg or Antietam, we being yet at Harper's Ferry. But we were ordered to the field, whither we went in rapid march, crossing the Potomac at Boteler's Ford, the water being hip deep. All wet and draggled we hurried on to the field of battle, and took position upon the Confed. right. Advancing through a cornfield, there suddenly rose before us a line of the enemy, whom we drove in disorder at the first fire.

Running rapidly forward through the corn, we stopped at the top of the hill and poured a galling fire into the fleeing foe. Many of them stopped in a little hollow in the corn at the foot of the hill, afraid to attempt the passage of the open slope beyond. Into them grouped here in a crouching disorderly line, we poured volley after volley, doubtless with terrible execution. I say volleys, and here was the only time in battle that I now remember firing to be done by command. Maj. Alston many times gave the command, "Right wing—ready—aim—fire—Load! Left wing—ready—aim—fire!—Load!" with splendid effect, for the line obeyed as a drill.

Besides those lying in the ravine, part of the enemy's line had taken refuge behind a stone fence or ridge of rocks which did not appear to protect them fully, for by ones and twos and threes they were continually breaking from it and fleeing across the open slope beyond. These with those who fled the ravine fairly dotted the green slope. And now amongst them, spurring down the hillside, came galloping an officer, mounted upon a black horse, waving his sword and endeavoring to rally the scattered line. Our eyes all turned to him, a fair mark, and half a thousand rifles were aimed, and a storm of bullets sped on their mission. Both horse and rider fell.

This scene and that of the Confederate charge at Cold Harbor, with the leader on horseback waving the flag—these two I remember as the brightest pictures of the war. Both were brave men, and I shall never cease to regret the eagerness on our part that did not spare so brave a man—although I still believe that it was the duty of every one of us to kill that particular man (for he was the most tremendous enemy we had).

Suddenly and unexpectedly, whilst we were thus having things our own way, came a volley from our flank which drove us back precipitately, and we had hardly chance to deliver a shot ere we were being hotly pursued. I found myself dropping behind; for my pantaloons (which I had found at Manassas Junction) proved to be of weak stuff and had already begun to rip at the bottom of the left leg. And now being wet by fording the river, they were heavier, so that running caused them to split further and further, so that now every time I threw the left leg forward, the breeches leg flew forward and wrapped around my right leg. Bullets whistled around me thick, for I must have been a conspicuous target. A bullet struck me on the right side of the head, leaving a black mark on my gray felt hat. Feeling it strike, I stopped, seized the cloth in my hands and tore the leg off a foot above the knee, and "skedaddled."

Our line did not run far, but jumped into a gully and fronted, awaiting in this natural breastwork the advance of the enemy. But they did not come, nor were we ordered forward. Sitting down there, one of the men asked me if that was a bullet hole in my drawers. Looking down I saw two holes near the bottom of the leg, and unrolling it (for they had been made for a good deal longer man than me) I found in all six holes, one bullet having doubtless passed through three folds of the cloth. And so I came out of the battle of Sharpsburg or Antietam half trouserless.

We remained upon the field the next day, the enemy although largely outnumbering us, not being in condition after the hard fighting of the 17th to renew the attack. But on the night of the 19th we recrossed the Potomac. If I remember rightly, our brigade was the last to cross, being rear guard. We marched into a wood and remained there quietly. On the morning of the 20th we were suddenly called to arms and marched hastily back toward the river. We soon heard fighting ahead of us, and we rightly conjectured that the enemy, presuming to attempt to cross the river in pursuit, was being met by Jackson.

Forming line of battle in the fields, we marched forward. When [we were] passing over a hill overlooking the river, a battery stationed on the other side opened upon us with shell, doing a good deal of damage. It was the best artillery shooting I ever saw. Every shell seemed to burst immediately in front of our line, the colors being the targets. I saw one shell burst in front of a Ga. regt. bringing down the colors and four men.

We lay down in a hollow behind a low hill awaiting orders to advance, while shrapnel & grape shot came rolling down the hill to where we lay, with every discharge from the enemy's guns. It was almost comic while lying down to see the balls come hopping and skipping and rolling down the hill. One bullet struck my brother a severe blow on the shoulder making a painful bruise. It would seem that the danger would have kept us awake; I suppose there is a somniferous influence in the sound. It was strange what a disposition there was in the men to go to sleep, lying down under this shelling.

We were not called into action, the enemy being effectually beaten without need of us. It seems that Jackson, waiting till enough had crossed for his purpose, had suddenly turned upon them and had driven them with great slaughter into the river, many being killed in the attempt to recross.

We now moved slowly up the Shenandoah Valley, that is, southward, halting sometimes for days together. It was while halted at Castleman's Ford opposite Snicker's Gap that finding some walnut trees, I collected a quantity of the nuts, extracted the kernels, mixed them with flour, and cooked the compound. My anticipations were high, and the first bite was rather enticing. But the third bite palled, and I saw I had ruined two days' rations. So I began smacking my lips, setting a trap for the boys. And into the trap they fell, every man anxious to taste.

"But if I give each one even a little taste, all my bread will be gone," I said.

The remedy for that was simple, of course. So as fast as I passed to one a small piece, he paid me with a piece of his own, as large, or generally—to be sure of doing the fair thing —a little larger. So in exchange for my uneatable walnut bread, I got somewhat more of common bread, albeit in more pieces. After that I ate my walnuts in the usual way.

We continued up the Valley by leisurely marches, say 16 to 20 miles a day, crossed the Blue Ridge at Luray Gap into the Luray Valley and on to Fredericksburg. When camped near Fredericksburg six months before, Bail and I used to go some distance to a little cottage amongst the hills where we would buy milk, and maybe butter or eggs, and where we had our clothes washed every week. We never came but the owner, Miss Stevens (white-haired, a quiet, gentle soul) had ready for us a bowl of sweet clabber. We got to be quite friends and she used to call us "*my* boys."

And now when camped again in the same neighborhood, I struck out one evening for Hamilton's crossing, near which her house stood. Recognizing me at once, Miss Stevens cried, "Where's the other one?"

"He was killed at Manassas." I think of the two of us, Bail must have been her favorite, from the grief she showed.

While encamped here, my brother took sick, and Miss Stevens was of great assistance, furnishing milk and other delicacies, when he could not eat camp fare. Blackwood grew worse rapidly, and in a short while he was down on his back in a tent, so ill that he could not raise himself in bed. The Dr. told me plainly that there was small hope of his recovery. I was detailed at my own request to nurse him. I tramped through the snow every day for milk, not leaving him else.

But one day while Blackwood was at his lowest, suddenly beat the long roll. The enemy were attempting to cross the river. I had to leave my brother and go. I bade him goodbye with as cheerful an air as I could muster, but I hardly hoped to see him ever again. This was Dec. 12, 1862, and snow lay on the ground.

We marched toward the river, forming line of battle along a military road that ran through the woods, and we camped there that night. The next day we may have shifted about a little, but we still kept position in the road, which ran parallel to the edge of the woods some distance in front. We had another line in front of us (at the edge of the woods) we being the second line-of-battle. We were ordered to stack arms in the road and lie down.

Lying in the woods behind our stacked arms, we underwent a heavy shelling, a good many men being wounded, some in our company. A man belonging to Co. E. lying close to me, had his arm shattered. Capt. Haskell, out in front of us, sitting with his back to the enemy, leaning against a sapling the size of a man's arm, quietly munched a cracker.

Suddenly there began to come mixed with the shells,

rifle balls. Faster and faster they came, and there was quite a stir on our right, where we could see men jumping up and seizing their guns, some beginning to fire.

We sprang to the stacks, but our officers shouted, "Let the guns alone! Lie down! Those are our men in front!"

Whish came the bullets, faster than ever. The commotion on our right increased, and far up to the right we could see our men jumping up and seizing their guns. Many were firing and loading as fast as they could, others stood irresolute, many officers in front trying to keep the men from firing.

We could stand it no longer. We all rose, and the officers then ordered us to take arms. We no sooner had them in hand than we saw men in front. Some cried, "They are Yankees!" and began firing. Others shouted: "No, they're our own men; don't shoot."

Then came the cry, "Forward!" My old schoolmate, Sergt. Pete Ransom, sprang forward on the left, heading the charge. Down the slope we went, firing, and driving whoever they were. But we did not drive far, being halted and ordered back.

All was hubbub, some saying, "They were Yankees, I tell you. I saw their blue clothes." Others said, "Couldn't be Yankees; there's a N. C. brigade out front; been there all the time."

Sergt. Mackey says: "Well, I hope they're not our men, for I've killed one." He was very pale, and plainly in great trouble lest he had killed one of our own men, for of the killing he was positive.

Then to know, a few men were sent down to the front to look at the dead. They soon returned with the good news that it was the enemy. Mackey's man they found dead just where he had said.

On the right, the trouble had been worse. The enemy through a gap between two brigades in our front had advanced in a line oblique to ours, striking our right first, which received the brunt of the meeting. When they first advanced, Gen. Gregg, being quite certain it was the first line of battle falling

back, rode in front of his men commanding them to cease
firing. And thereby he lost his life, for the enemy came quickly
upon him and he was shot from his horse by a single soldier,
receiving a wound from which he died. How it was that the
line which was in our front got out of position, exposing us
to surprise, I don't think was ever clearly explained.

During the battle—just after our charge while we were
down in the woods in a state of considerable excitement—a
rabbit jumped up and ran here and there among the men,
seemingly frightened out of its wits. And no wonder, for
in all directions it heard the rattle of small arms, and the roar
of artillery and bursting of shells. In its imagination no doubt
it was the last grand hunt of the world, a very Judgment Day.
Finally the poor creature jumped up on a stump just in front
of the line and squatted there, the most conspicuous position
it could possibly have found.

When the fighting was over some of us went down in
the woods to give relief to the wounded enemy. Some we gave
water and did not move; others we moved off to some fires
that had been built; and to one I gave my blanket as he lay
off in the cold by himself. We moved a young fellow who said
he was a Pennsylvanian, 18 years old, to a good fire where we
had quite a party of them collected. I asked him would he
fight us again. He replied viciously, "Yes, I will."

Moving through the woods next day, we saw the trees
spotted and scored with the marks of bullets, most of them
just overhead, which shows that the average aim is too high.
In one tree we found a ramrod which had been shot into
it, and wonderfully bent and twisted it was. No one was strong
enough to pull it out.

Our fight was only a small episode in the great battle of
Fredericksburg, the heavy portion of which was fought some
distance to our left, we being on the right of the army.

Decr. 16th we returned to camp, packed up and marched
about 6 miles. The camp we now took up was about 2 miles
from the river (Rappahannock) upon which near Moss Neck
Church we picketed. This was some 8 or 10 miles below

Fredericksburg. We now went into winter quarters, putting up various kinds of structures, each mess according to its fancy; but there were very few, if any, houses such as were put up at Suffolk the winter before.

The most substantial structures were the "Merrimacs." To make them, two heavy forks of trees were posted in the ground, and across the forks was laid a stout horizontal pole. Leaning against this pole were set other poles or fence rails, the lower ends resting on the ground. The roof thus formed was covered first with leaves, then with earth on top of the leaves. One end was generally closed by bushes wattled together or poles driven in the ground; the front being sometimes left open, sometimes closed by an old blanket or oilcloth. To give more room, some of the men set such a structure or tent over a square hole in the ground, from two to four feet deep. Some of the officers' quarters, perhaps most of them, were made so.

Shortly after we stopped here, Blackwood came marching up to camp, in fine spirits. And you may be sure I was rejoiced to see him, for I did not know whether he was alive or dead. All I knew was that from camp where I had left him, to go into battle, he had been moved to hospital in Richmond. In the hospital, his recovery from so low a state was rapid.

Blackwood and I had a couple of flies, which when put up together made a very comfortable tent for two, one end closed by bushes wattled together, the other with an oilcloth. Such, with a floor of poles laid close together and raised a foot or so off the ground, was our house during the winter of 1862-3. Our bed was of broomstraw, which I always preferred to wheat straw, as not breaking up so badly. In severe weather our cloth house was cold, but generally we made out well enough, and it was a rare thing to have a cold.

Water we got from a stream bordered on each side by swamp, so that a corduroy road had to be constructed across it, with a bridge of poles. On the hills on one side were camped North Carolina men; on the other, ourselves, South Carolinians. And now there was a great deal of snowballing, the officers themselves often getting well pelted. From fighting amongst ourselves, it got to be quite common for one regiment to attack another. Usually we stormed the camp of one of the regiments close by, and a hard task it was to climb the steep hill under a shower of snowballs.

During this winter, there was much gambling. Efforts to suppress it were unsuccessful. The gamblers hid in the depths of the forest and generally managed to elude the search guards that were sent out on patrol. One part of the forest was commonly known by the name of the popular game, "chuck-a-luck" woods.

Around the camp fires, we found that heat aggravated the insects which latterly had come to be constant traveling companions, every man's clothes (be he man or officer) being populated with them. We had dignified them with the name of greybacks; time was when they were called bodylice. Another great trouble of this kind was the camp-itch, which was dreadful, and extended almost entirely throughout the army, though my brother and I never had it. Of diseases, the most prevalent were measles and mumps, especially the former, of which many died. Fortunately Blackwood and I had had both when children. The lice we hadn't had and they broke out on us.

We picketed the Rappahannock at Moss Neck Church, one's turn to picket coming every few days, 24 hours being the term. We became quite friendly with the enemy's pickets posted on the opposite side, and used to talk with them and exchange newspapers. The exchange was made by taking a piece of board or bark, fixing a stick upright in it as a mast, with the paper attached to this as a sail. By setting the sail properly, the wind would carry it across from one side to the other, as it was wanted to go. Once a Federal band came down to the river and played "Dixie." We cheered them vociferously, of course. Then it played "Yankee Doodle," and the enemy cheered. Then "Home, Sweet Home," and the cheer went up loud and long from both sides of the river.

One day on picket at an old barn, where there were a good

many rats, some of the boys in jest proposed to catch some and see how they would eat, broiled. But the jest was changed to earnest, and soon some were killed and on the coals, and given a trial, Blackwood being one of the ring leaders. They gave it as their opinion that rat tasted like young squirrel, and the rest of us took their word for it. If that time were back, I don't think I would now be squeamish. I overcame my prejudice against the bullfrog, and found him very nice. On the margin of the river grew great beds of calamus, which some of the boys were fond of chewing, though I never liked it. My diary of Feb. 2/63 reads: "Eat my whole day's ration at one meal. Slim, very slim. But half a loaf is better than no bread. We enjoy ourselves well for all that—are full of hope, conscious of our ability to cope with our enemy and look to the next thrashing we give them as the harbinger of peace."

When spring came, the river some distance below us was fished regularly by a detail appointed for the purpose, and shad were caught by wagon loads and issued to the troops as rations. Another luxury we began to enjoy was tea—spicewood tea. The spicewood bush grows here along the streams, and the young buds and leaves make a very fragrant tea, something like sassafras.

Long before winter was over, the woods had all been cut down for fuel. First the smaller trees, then the larger, until only here and there could be seen one standing, the largest of all. And when these were felled, the stumps were cut over again level with the ground, and men coming in from picket would be seen carrying logs of wood to camp, maybe two miles distance. So the whole country presented a dreary scene of hills covered over with huts, tents, "Merrimacs," flies, all kinds of soldiers' habitation, and no tree nor bush for shelter, and no grass, all dusty and grey beneath. A deserted camp of this kind presents a scene of utter desolation. And after the stumps were gone? Ah, then we dug up roots. And then? Wood was hauled on wagons from a distance and issued as rations. I will not say positively, however, that at this time we got beyond the roots. But we *have* had wood issued as rations, small rations too.

In the last of April 1863, Hooker began his forward movement, crossing above the Confederates' left and massing about Chancellorsville in the Wilderness. Thither we marched to meet him, doing some little skirmishing before getting in good striking distance.

It was now that with 20,000 men under Jackson we made the famous flank movement, falling upon Hooker's right wing. Stealthily we went on our mission, a line of skirmishers marching on the right, a good way from the column, and cavalry outside these. Ways were chosen to avoid being seen by the enemy. At the outset we were seen by a Federal post of artillery on a distant hill in the forest, and shelled. Once we were fired on by sharpshooters at a long distance. Passing over hills, we skulked behind bushes, walking sometimes half bent and with trailed arms. Once we saw a balloon which the enemy had sent up, and I hardly think its occupants could have failed to see us. The line coming to rest in a little field in a hollow, I washed my face for the first time in three days.

Coming out to the Plank Road, we here fell suddenly upon the enemy, coming upon them unawares while they were cooking. The assault fell not only upon their flank but rear, so they had to jump their breastworks and fight from the wrong side. In this surprise, our brigade had no active part, however.

I will now quote from my diary: "About dark, while marching in column, a terrific fire of shells was opened upon us. The full moon was shining brightly and objects were visible at a good distance. The shells came like skyrockets, leaving a long curved line of fire and bursting all around us. About 9 or 10 o'clock we halted, stacked arms in the road, and were ordered to bivouac to the rear of the stacks.

"We had hardly spread our blankets when a sudden volley in our front startled us, and we rushed to our arms. The firing kept up; the battle was being continued by moonlight. We were the second line, and were ordered forward. Our march was obstructed by the small pines which formed a dense thicket, through which we could hardly work our way. Then we were ordered to lie down. After a little the battle ceased and we were ordered back to the Road. But not allowed to rest many minutes, for we were again marched down the Road, filed to the right and stopped a while. Before I could get to sleep we were ordered on. Filing again into the thicket, we formed the first line of battle. Meanwhile there had been several other small engagements in our front. I slept some now.

"At daylight Sunday, May 3/63 our skirmishers were ordered forward, we following in line of battle. Soon the shots in front told the presence of the enemy, and we pressed on, keeping as good a line as possible in the dense undergrowth. The battle now became general on our right.

"Directly we crossed a narrow marsh, in front of which was a cleared space. Coming into this open ground, we saw just ahead a line of breastworks, and far beyond in the woods a few straggling bluecoats running. They had probably been flanked. We met with no opposition at the entrenchments— the enemy had fled. But not so on the right, for after we had crossed, I could see the enemy still at their breastworks fighting well.

"We now found ourselves in a perfect maze of boughs placed by the enemy to impede our progress. Marching up a slope (still in the woods) we arrived at the top of a low hill, and here we received a hot fire of infantry and artillery. We halted and became engaged. I had fired some half dozen shots when I felt a blow on my left leg, just above the ankle. Stooping down to see, I found my stocking filling with blood. I turned to my captain, with whom I had just been talking. He asked was I wounded, and I told him I was. He ordered me at once to the rear.

"Using my gun as a crutch, I hobbled back, passing many dead and disabled. At a road a little way back I met up with two of our company, Hurley, who was shot in the shoulder, and Clarke, shot in the leg. Hurley was in great pain, his arm being broken. Clarke and I cut his equipments off his shoulders, and we three hobbled off together, holding to each other, still in danger of being wounded again, as the bullets were coming thick.

"After resting two or three times, we at last got out of range of the bullets and reached a spot where the wounded of our Regt. were being collected, and where I found one or two others of the Co. After having my wound dressed, I was taken off with Clarke in an ambulance to the Division Hospital, which was simply an old field (the battlefield of the day before, in fact) with such shelter as could be provided in the way of tent flies and brush arbors. Parnell, one of our Co., had a fly which was soon stretched for him, Clarke and myself."

There was another of our Co. here wounded; and close by on a table lay Lt. Proctor, a young nephew of Gen. Beauregard, who had run away from school to join the army. He had attached himself to Gen. Gregg, and his first battle was Fredericksburg. And now he was shot in the leg, which had to be amputated. He took it coolly, smoking a cigar while the surgeons performed the operation. Lying here, we listened to the roar of the battle, which gradually grew fainter, as did the yells of the Confederates, so we knew that our men were still driving the enemy and that the victory was ours. But we had lost Jackson, struck down by our own men, in that volley which had made us jump so quick the night before.

Never more would we follow him to battle, never again would he be cursed by his own men for his hard marching, never again so wildly cheered by the same men as he galloped by them. For I have heard men, worn out by a break-neck march, cursing Jackson bitterly, yet all the while they worshipped him, and could not have been bribed to drop out of ranks.

Of the times I have heard him cheered, I will tell of two. It was just after the battle of Sharpsburg. Having crossed back into Virginia, we were marched to the B. & O. R. R., which we burnt for a long distance, destroying the telegraph also, cutting down the posts and tangling up the wires. We had torn up the road and burnt it and were marching back. Stopping to rest in the woods, we stacked arms just on the side of the road and lay down.

While lying here, we heard a faint yell in the distance, back on the road. The men began to say: "Jackson or a rabbit; Jackson or a rabbit."

The yell continuing and growing louder and nearer, everybody says, "It's Jackson! It's Jackson!"

Directly came the sound of horse's feet galloping. Then as all men rose, waving hats in the air and cheering the rider, came Jackson at a furious gallop, looking neither to the right nor to the left, not even paying the least heed to a stand of arms belonging to my company that stood in the road, but riding over them, scattering them right and left. After him, some fifty yards behind came his aides, trying to keep him in sight. I have often thought that of all relics of the war, I would rather have the gun that his horse's hoof struck just then than any other.

"Jackson or a rabbit!" That was the cry always made when a distant yell was heard, for whether one or the other, no pair of eyes would ever rest on him, but the mouth under them opened and gave vent to a prolonged yell. They were both cheered the same, only Jackson with "hats off."

The other time I speak of was at Harper's Ferry. We were all occupied at one thing or another, just after the surrender, the prisoners moving freely amongst us, though well guarded, when the cry was heard and the clattering hoofs.

"What's the matter?" asked the prisoners.

"Jackson's coming!" was the answer.

All feet rushed to the road, and such a cheer as was set up by men in grey and men in blue has seldom been heard. For the prisoners all cheered him just as lustily and heartily as we did ourselves. And we felt very kindly toward them for it.

And now Jackson lay mortally wounded, his brilliant story drawing to a close. As I lay in my hospital cot in Manchester, I heard the bells of Richmond tolling his death. Such gloom therefor as fell upon the people! For the valiantest soldier of the land lay dead.

☆ 3 ☆

I Miss Gettysburg

INVALIDED HOME — BLACKWOOD'S LETTERS — BACK TO WAR

☆ ☆ ☆ ☆ ☆ ☆ ☆ ☆ ☆ ☆ ☆

ON THE morning of May 4th, I was helped into a wagon in which were three others of the Regt. We drove off but had gone but a little distance when the whole train was halted, Gen. Lee having ordered that the wagons (which belonged to the Commissary Dept.) should immediately load with arms and proceed to Guinness Station. We were taken out and returned to the field hospital. Word was sent to the Genl. that the wagons were about to take off the wounded, and he revoked his order. We got in again and after having been jolted over stones and stumps for 25 miles, reached the station a little after dark. There were many wounded collected here. I slept on a pile of ammunition boxes in a freight car.

Next morning, with some help I got into a car which was already crowded, and at 11 A.M. the train moved off. I was in a small square boxcar without a roof. As we were getting ready to start, all the soldiers, teamsters, and others that could be got together, were armed and drawn up to resist an expected attack on the station.

At Hanover Junction we staid all night, the track between there and Richmond having been torn up by a body of the enemy's cavalry, who had made a raid in our rear. A thunder storm came up and the rain continued till near midday the next day. I did not get wet, having a rubber cloth. But I got no sleep, having to sit up on the edge of the box car wall all the time. We arrived in Richmond May 6th and were

41

taken to the Receiving and Distributing hospital, where we remained till next day.

On May 7th, by paying $10 for a hack, three of us—Sergeants Martin and Force of Co. L. and myself—were transferred to the South Carolina Hospital in Manchester. Had my wound dressed for the second time since being wounded. Manchester Hospital had for inmates South Carolina men, perhaps exclusively, and was presided over by a surgeon from Charleston. The building was formerly used as a tobacco factory. My wound improved, and before the month was out, I could hobble around on a crutch. Of an evening we used to crowd around the front windows and watch the girls go by, and a great treat it was after a winter in quarters and part of a campaign.

A little girl, Lily Rosalie Pilkington, of Manchester, Va. used to come into our hospital nearly every day, bringing bunches of flowers and singing for us. She was four or five years old, and could sing sweetly, having a fine voice. She was petted by all, and there was no eye that did not brighten at her coming. She was a great comfort to us, and it was with real sorrow that I received a letter from her father after the war, telling of her death.

One morning, hobbling out to breakfast on my crutch, I got a bad fall. It had rained the night before, so that the raised plank platform over which we had to walk to breakfast in another building had become wet and slippery. No sooner had I set the end of my crutch upon it than it shot out from under me, and I fell, my crippled leg coming under me.

My wound was three inches above the ankle, the bullet having struck on the outside, passing between the skin and the bone in front. It must have rubbed the bone pretty hard; it was the barest possible escape from having my leg shattered.

Manchester Hospital being discontinued, I was transferred to Howard Grove Hospital on the edge of Richmond, and there in the same ward with me I found Hurley, whose arm had been amputated. He lay on a cot not far from mine, and every now and then he would bring his right arm across his body as though to take hold of something. Laughing, he said he felt as though his left arm were hanging down by the side of the cot, and involuntarily he would bring his right arm across to raise it. He said he could feel all the fingers of the lost hand.

Hurley was an excellent soldier, an Irishman by birth. He had been in the English army, and had fought in the Crimea. He said he had witnessed the charge of the famous "Six Hundred." Before coming to our war, he was engaged to be married to a South Carolina girl, but the girl's father didn't like it. Later when he went home with one arm off, the woman's soul rode roughshod over everything, and she married him in spite of every remonstrance.

On June 1st I received transfer to Augusta Hospital. The following from my diary was written on the cars going home, and the writing shows the rocking of the cars: "June 2, 1863, Started for home early in the morning. Left Petersburg 10 A.M., arrived at Weldon in the evening. Reached Wilmington just after sunrise on the 3rd. Train crowded at first, but by this time have plenty of room. Have some difficulty in changing cars at the connections. Have been feeling ill ever since I started and at Weldon I had fever. My wound in sad need of being dressed."

I reached Augusta in the afternoon of June 4th, reporting at the Hospital, which was then in the old Eagle and Phoenix Hotel building on Broad Street, Drs. Ford and Doughty superintending. I believe I was kept at the hospital a few days, being ill, my wound inflamed by the journey. Dr. Ford then gave me permission to go home, with orders to report at the hospital every day or two. In place of my old wooden crutch, I had bought a comfortable pair from Platt's and on these I hobbled about a long time before I could bear my weight on my foot.

At home, our fare was extremely plain, being chiefly bread, bacon, rice, hominy, sorghum, and such vegetables as the garden afforded. For coffee, rye was used. I have seen salt on the table quite brown in color, being made by boiling the earth dug up in smoke houses and evaporating the water. The table was often as scantily as it was plainly spread. For a while we made two meals a day do, at best having a little bread and milk for the children's supper. Clothes too were considered for economy's sake, bought with reference to wear rather than appearance. I think there were few whom the war did not bear heavily upon, and I do not know what many would have done had not the women been able to take in sewing from the Government, which gave out uniforms and underclothing for the soldiers, to be made. The pay for the work was small, but it helped keep the wolf from the door. And this resource added, no doubt, something of warmth and comfort to our own home during that splendid, troublous time.

I have omitted to mention that before this my father had moved from Hamburg, S. C. across the Savannah River to Augusta, Ga., having rented a house on Reynolds St. from Major S. H. Oliver, quartermaster of the post. Major Oliver was an old citizen who with his family now lived a stone's throw from us, on Broad St. His son, Geo. L. Oliver, about Blackwood's age, now came home, wounded both in the hand and the head. As he could walk about, it was but a little while before we had fallen in with each other. He took me round to his home and introduced me to his two sisters, Jeanie Oliver and Florida. My visits to the house were pretty frequent after that, my calls always being on Miss Florida. Jeanie Oliver seemed to fight shy of me. I think she considered me a rather insipid, uninteresting person. What she thinks of me now, after we have been married nine years, I am not prepared to say.

My connection with the army being severed as to action, grew closer in thought. With greed I followed, in the daily news, the march of the Army of Northern Virginia, my very soul burning more hotly to be with it. And when news of the battle of Gettysburg came, I felt as though I had sustained a loss that I could never regain. Yes, I feel so yet! I still lament that I was not at Gettysburg.

In a letter now lost Blackwood told me of the organization of a battalion of Sharpshooters from the Brigade, men picked for their courage and other good soldierly qualities. This body was placed in the hands of Capt. Haskell, doing the skirmishing, scouting, and most of the picketing for the Brigade. Although not intended to do so, it rarely could be so well kept together in pitched battles as to prevent its members from going headlong into a charge with the line of battle. In this command, Blackwood filled a Sergeant's position, though being but a private in actual rank.

I think I would better give now extracts from Blackwood's letters received during my stay at home:

"Bivouac somewhere in Penna. June 29, 1863— . . . We did not go to Winchester, but passed through Berryville and Shepherdstown, crossing at Boteler's Ford, then through Sharpsburg, Hagerstown and several other places. . . . Capt. Haskell's brother, Langdon, says we go to Gettysburg. The Corps will separate, and we will do splendidly, I hope. . . .

"Bivouac between Hagerstown and Williamsport, Md. July 7, 1863. "Dear Brother: Gettysburg!!! 'Twas an awful place, *four* days of volleyed thunder, the worst you ever heard tell of, and I guess it makes a fellow *feel* safe to be away from the place. . . . On the first of the month we (Pender's Division) debouched from our camp on the mountains and marched toward the town of Gettysburg, now of immortal memory. In the first place, you must know that the Sharpshooting Battalion always marches in front of the Brigade. I was acting 2nd Sergt. in it before the battle. We marched four miles, I suppose, and heard cannonading in front. Skirmishing. Heth's Division engaged. I believe our brigade was the extreme right. Haskell's Sharpshooters deployed. We marched in a line perpendicular to the brigade, covering it and guarding it from the Yankee Cavalry. Finally we (the Sharpshooters are *we*) flanked to the right and marched forward a mile and a half, leaving the brigade to take care of itself. All this time a battle was progressing on our left.

"We halted in sight of some of the enemy's cavalry and

sent out 3 or 4 men with an officer (or vice versa) and they ran the enemy's outpost away and took about 30 head of cattle and a horse and a *pig*! By this time a tremendous battle was raging on our left, but we were out of danger.

"About an hour later, Capt. Haskell gave a note to Lieut. Sharp telling him to send some reliable man from the Co. to Gen. Pender, with this report. Sharp studied a moment, then said 'Capt. I reckon Sgt. Benson will do!'

" 'Yes, Benson will find him,' replied the captain, and off I had to go.

"About three miles distant, I could see some large houses on fire. Inquiring my way, I found it led past them, in fact, between two of them. I went on, passing numbers of wounded men and dead horses, and presently came to Pettigrew's Brigade. I asked a man on a horse who (the man, not the horse) had three stars on his collar, where General Pender was. He said, 'Over there,' pointing to the left.

"I did not like it much, for a few shells and bullets were singing and moaning 'Over there,' but I had to go in and bear it. So I went on and found some dead and wounded men of the 13th, by which I knew our Brigade had been engaged, but I was afraid to ask if it had suffered much.

"I found Pender by himself, handed him the note, and was told, 'Tell the Capt. to bring his men in.' It was late in the afternoon, so I knew the battle was over for the day (our boys having already thrashed the Yankees decently), and it was night when we got to where I left Pender, and after a little more shelling we went to the Brigade.

"Our Brigade distinguished itself very much. It charged the Yankees behind a stone fence, and through the town. Our Regt. took two flags and a battery, I believe. Larkin and Jones (they say) were mortally wounded. Josey, Wilson, Godfrey, Jim Rourk, and Crosby, slightly. We slept somewhere a little of the night, our battalion being on duty, and next morning began skirmishing. Our company (C) was held in reserve. And we all threw up little Gibraltars for ourselves, and were shelled pretty fiercely during the day.

"Now I'm coming to the bad part of it. Some time during the day Sergt. Rhodes came down to where I was, and I could tell by the look of his eyes that something was the matter. He said, 'Benson, Capt. Haskell is killed.'

"I couldn't say anything. I saw his body borne past. He was shot under the arm and killed instantly by one of the enemy's sharpshooters.

"Late in the afternoon our company was ordered out. Lt. Poag of Co. A was in command, Maj. McCreery commanding the Regt. A little after dusk, we heard that Longstreet had come up; we had heard them fighting far to the right that afternoon. The enemy was in a splendid 'posish' on a high hill commanding the country for nearly a mile, and I think he must have had forty cannons there.

"A little after dark we received the order that Ramseur's Brigade was going ahead and we must not fire. I suppose it was intended to make a night attack on the hill, but the order was counter-manded and Ramseur's Brigade came back. It left pickets in advance of ours, and Lt. Sharp was ordered to join the left of his pickets with the right of Ramseur's. We went forward to the point designated, and could not find the picket from Ramseur's Brigade. The moon was up, but the sky was overcast with clouds. We were in a wheatfield where we might stumble upon the enemy before we knew it. I was the left, and Sharp ordered me to go forward and see if I could find the picket.

"There was a fence nearby, running in the direction I was to take, with once in a while a small bush growing beside it. It answered my purpose very well. I had followed it about 50 yards when I saw a line of skirmishers on both sides of the fence, about 75 yards ahead. I could not see them plainly, so I got on my belly and *snaked* it about 25 yards farther, and came to a halt. I saw they were dressed in dark clothes, and I felt that if they were Yankees they could take me if I went farther. So I crawled back to the Lt. and told him about it. He told me to go back and ask them who they were.

"I went back very cautiously and got about 50 yards

from them, when (as well as I can remember) the following occurred:

BENSON: (in loud voice) 'Whose pickets are those?'

REPLY: '*Our* pickets.'

 The 'our' *sounded* Confederate; a pause of about a minute ensued.

BENSON: 'To which side do you belong?'

REPLY: 'Whose side are *you* on?'

BENSON: 'The Rebels.'

REPLY: 'Well, we are for the Union.'

"I dried up for five minutes and then shouted, 'Are those the pickets from Gen. Ramseur's Brigade?'—No answer but a couple of shots, and their necessary appendage, the whistle. Presently I asked the same question again and received for answer, 'Who *are* you, anyhow?' very near me, so near that I thought he must be in 20 yards of me. I did not say anything more, but crawled back to the company, which I found had fallen back a little, and who thought I was taken.

"Next day we had it hot. The Yankee skirmishers charged us several times and were driven back. They took possession of a large barn on our right, and commenced firing from the windows. The first shot killed Sergt. Rhodes. Our flank being exposed, our artillery fired the barn. The very heaviest and most rapid artillery firing *anybody* ever heard. We retreated. So did the enemy. Hilton slightly wounded; Vogt wounded in the hand. Co. C. lost Lt. Poag, killed. Capt. Shooter in command of Sharpshooters.

         Your brother, B. K. Benson."

Altho' our army was repulsed at Gettysburg, there was not the slightest feeling of defeat amongst the men. Blackwood says the morale was perfect, and that they were never in finer spirits than the day after. [But subsequent letters like the following tell of additional hardships]:

"Near Culpepper C. H., July 24, 1863. Dear Berry: I've gone and done got 'barefeeted,' as Betty used to say. Kiss her and Callie for me. Well, old hoss, we have had another *turr*ible march, and nobody knows whether it's over yet.

Yesterday (it seems) we were at Gettysburg and now we're here. Let me give you an incident or two that occurred in the battle or skirmish at Falling Waters, where we crossed the Potomac on our retreat.

"We were all lying asleep, waiting for the troops to cross, when the enemy's cavalry—some three or four hundred thousand in number—came galloping up to us (probably thinking they would raise a party of stragglers, like they had been doing all morning) and got in amongst us before anybody was awake hardly. Two or three hand-to-hand fights occurred. One of the Infernal (or Infirmary) Corps, was ordered to surrender, and not seeing fit to do so, picked up a fence rail and slammed Mr. Yankee's life out of him. The men's guns were wet, and a great many refused to fire. (The guns, not the men.) One cavalryman (or *boy* they say he was) rode up to one of our men who had just discharged his piece, and ordered him to surrender. Our man refusing, the horseman charged upon him with drawn sabre. But our chap knocked him dead off his horse with the butt of his gun. I fired at a horseman charging with drawn sabre in less than fifty yards of me—and missed him! But somebody else didn't. The Yankees had the Sharpshooters nearly surrounded once, and had it not been for a piece of thick woods we would all have been taken. Ten of us were captured.

"The men like Capt. Barnwell very well now. Every day they like him better. He outshone everyone else I saw at Falling Waters. When I saw him he was 'footback,' with no sword, and a gun on his shoulder, trying to straighten out the line, which seemed to me in inextricable confusion. The Brigade was just going to cross the river, and the bridge being in sight and the Yankee Sharpshooters piling into our rear, naturally everyone in the main line wanted to get over as quickly as possible. Barnwell somehow or other succeeded in getting the line into *splendid order.* . . .

"I don't believe you know who is in command of the Brigade. Col. Abner Perrin of the 14th has been ever since we left camp at Fredericksburg. He acted well at Gettysburg. At the commencement of the charge that won the battle of the first day, he rode forward waving his sword and shouted 'Three cheers for Gregg's Brigade!' and went into it all over. . . .

"I noticed a piece about our regiment in a late Charleston *Mercury*. It says that the 1st has lost in killed and wounded 700 out of 900. There have been 14 officers killed in the Regt. Many of the officers twice wounded. Also that our Regt. has suffered more severely in action than any other Regt. from our state, unless it be Orr's Rifles, and you know the 'rifles' is nearly twice as large a Regt. as ours. Our company draws 19 rations. While we were retreating through Maryland, I have known it to have only 5 men besides Segt. Mackey.

"The Brigade gained a very good name for the gallantry with which it fought at Gettysburg. Capt. Barnwell says he thinks it made the best charge that had been made during the war, and our regiment was foremost in the charge. . . . Everybody says that Peagler is the best man of the Ambulance Corps, and he is not modest enough to deny it. He says so as well as the others. . . . Capt. Butler and Lt. Owens went to South Carolina a few days ago to bring back stragglers from the army. Other Regts. in the Brigade are doing the same."

"Camp near Orange Court House, Aug. 15, 1863. . . . Since we have been living here we have had a variety of viands. Sometimes they give us bacon and sometimes beef; sometimes meal and sometimes flour; sometimes salt and sometimes none. Once in a long while a little sugar. We have had several blackberry pies, and lately lots of green corn. Two ears of corn are issued as a ration. I blame Lee very much for starting off with us on this campaign before the corn was fit to eat. He ought never to have thought of taking us into a strange and foreign land without waiting for the only means of subsistence to become fit to eat. But no, he carries us off, and the first thing we know we are without rations and no corn! Lee's usual foresight and sagacity failed him that pop, certain. But he wouldn't take my advice. . . . Seriously, we don't like the retreat from Pennsylvania, a bit. Lee tried to make us take a mountain, and because we couldn't do it, he runs back into Virginia. I don't think we were whipped bad enough to abandon the ground just because Meade had a good position."

"Orange Court House, Sept 15, 1863. Dear Brother: We are expecting a battle. The whole corps except Wilcox's Division is in line. . . . We hear the most extravagant rumors. . . . One is that the enemy is crossing at Ely's Ford, some twenty miles below, in three columns! Just imagine three columns crossing at one small ford at the same time. . . . Later—The alarm is over. It turned out to be only an armed reconnaisance. . . . Has Longstreet's Corps gone west? We say so, and I firmly believe it has."

"Orange C. H., Va.
Nov. 16
"Dear Bro.: The 1st S. C. and 12th Ga. started on Nov. 2nd from Brandy and marched to Flint Hill (a small place in Rappahannock County) to hunt deserters and conscripts, and we staid in the mountains, marching south, for about 10 days. Together we captured nearly 200 persons including 8 or 10 Yankees. . . . We had a very good time amongst the mountains. Pretty arduous, tho', toiling over the hills all day. When we would take a man out of his house, the feminines would get outrageous. I had to take a man from amongst a parcel of women who cried like anything when they heard he had to go. . . . All we disliked our trip for was the heavy guard duty we had to do on account of so many prisoners."

"Orange C. H. Va. Dec. 4th
"Dear Bro.: I suppose you have heard of Meade's advance and retreat, and all about it. No one hurt in our company. We had a tough, cold time of it, and we were very glad Meade did retreat. We got back here in our old camp yesterday. . . .

"You want to know my 'earthly possessions and the condition they are in'. —One hat in tolerable order; one overcoat; 2 pieces of carpet (one good, one burnt); 2 pieces of tent fly (both burnt, one patched); 2 pairs of shoes (one good, one bad); 1 knapsack; 1 worn haversack; 4 shirts; 1 drawers; 1 pants; 1 cup; 1 fork; 2 halves of a Yankee canteen for plates; and that's about all except my gun and harness. . . . Lice are not very plentiful, because we all wage a war of extermination against them. Still, if you want to see one, we can show it. . . . When you come, bring as much soap as you conveniently can. Bring some pounded red pepper. The men say bring 6 lbs. soda. Rations are scarce now; they are one day behind. I think I can catch up though, for I bought some rice yesterday. Bring some needles and thread if you can. This is the only pen and ink in the company and Miller wants it to make out pay rolls with, so I'll quit. B.K.B."

Off to the wars again! Leaving home early on the morning of Dec. 2, 1863, I reached Petersburg Dec. 5th and spent that night at Howard Grove, visiting my cousin, Zack Benson. Reached Orange C. H. late afternoon of Dec. 6th. Walked 3 miles to camp, my leg giving trouble, having been injured on the way.

I remember very well on going through the camps, before reaching my own, being hailed with continuous cries of "Hospital Rat! Hospital Rat!" About hospitals, just as they do about hotels and such places, rats always collected in numbers, big ones, and got fat off stealings and waste, of course, and as there were some men who shirked the camp and the campaign, and, under pretense of being sick, spent a large portion of their time at hospitals, the good soldiers conceived a natural hearty dislike and contempt for these, and applied to them the epithet of Hospital Rat, as implying their having made the hospital a permanent abode. But as soldiers are not very discriminating in their judgments, or rather, because the temptation to fling a stone is too enticing, they seldom stopped to inquire whether the passerby really deserved the name or not; the wearing of clean clothes without holes in them was evidence, which, although it might be merely circumstantial, was to them strong enough to warrant the attack. Private or officer, he could not escape the shelling, and many's the man who, having arrived close to his camp early in the evening, has hung around in the woods till dusk, before venturing to run the gantlet: "Hospital Rat! Hospital Rat!"

The men were busy building winter quarters. Our company frequently had picket duty on the Rapidan. My diary states that on Dec. 23rd Co. H. "has eleven men and 1 officer for picket duty," and that on Christmas Day we had as "Ration of meat today ¼ lb. salt beef," and further that I "Sent to the mill and bought ½ bushel of meal, price $8.00."

During my absence, some new men had been added to the company, some of them volunteers, others conscripts. "Conscript" was a rough name to bear; and it would have been natural had the men bearing it behaved less gallantly than the others, but I must say that generally speaking, they did well. There were some whom we learned to call among our best soldiers.

When we first went into the army, we had scales for weighing, and measures for liquids, but long before this time the commissary of a company was reduced to dividing out to the men in a much more primitive fashion whatever rations were received from the Regimental Commissary. The meat (usually bacon) was divided carefully into as many "piles" as there were men, a "pile" usually being one little flat piece about the size of a small cake of toilet soap. Having arranged the "piles" on a log, the commissary would get some fair-minded member of the company to review with him their comparative values. Some such colloquy as this would then take place:

"Don't you think this here piece is a *little* too big?"

"W-e-e-ll, maybe it is. Where'll I cut it?"

"About there."

"Now where'll I put the scrap?"

"Put her over here with *this* feller; it's end and about the littlest one you got. But, I say, here's a right smart sized chunk; don't you think it's too big?"

"Well, I don't know; she *looks* pretty big, but if you'll notice she's got a dog-gone sight of bone in her."

"Yes, she *has* got a good deal of bone. Well, let her rip!" Commissary now bawls, "Come up men and get your meat!"

The men gather round in an irregular semi-circle of which the meat is the focus, all eyes fastened on the piece "with a dog-gone sight of bone in her." Then the commissary says, "Well, who's a-goin' to call?"

Nobody answers. A pause. Then the commissary says, "How in the hell am I a-goin' to give you your meat if nobody ain't a-goin' to call?"

One speaks up: "Well, I'll call if nobody else won't." He walks off about three paces and turns his back.

The commissary, touching a "pile" with his knife, asks, "Whose is this?"

"White's." White takes it up and retires, balancing it up and down in his hand.

"Whose is this?"

"Mister Peagler's." And so on until all are taken, and the little crowd disperses.

Flour, rice, meal, sugar etc. were divided by measure. Knowing by experience that one man's ration measured about so much in his cup or so many spoonfuls, the commissary called the men up one at a time, giving each his ration as near as he could guess, but taking care not to give too much. This care lest the supply give out before the end was reached, necessarily caused him to give too little, so that there would still be something left. This was called the "over-plus," or in camp dialect, the "overplush." Then the voice of the commissary was heard in the land: "Come up, men, and get your over-plush." And when this was divided it not unfrequently happened that a little was still left. But to share in this second "overplush," some of the high and mighty, the proud ones of the earth, disdained, replying to the commissary's summons, "Go to hell with your second overplush."

On Jan. 22, 1864 our company was on picket at Barnett's Ford. My diary notes that on that date "Strength of Co. for duty was 1 commissioned officer, 2 non comd. officers, 8 privates."

Because of a growing scarcity of wood, it was decided to change the site of our camp. Quoting from my diary: "Jan. 27, 1864—Went to work in the new camp. Labored hard, carrying poles, putting them up as the frame of the house. We are building a house for 5, a recruit being expected."

I think the four men for whom we were building a house were Owens, Rice, Blackwood, and myself, the recruit expected being our cousin Zack Benson, who wanted to go into service as soon as he could get his father's permission. The size of the house when finished was about 12 feet square, being built entirely of logs, chinked with clay. The chimney was built of split wood, chinked with clay the same as the house, but having a thick coat of clay inside to prevent taking fire. The protection, however, was but partial, so that there was hardly a day in the winter but somebody's chimney was on fire in the camp. Some of the quarters were the oddest little structures, which could hardly be entered on all fours. A passer-by could tiptoe and spit down the chimney. It wasn't at all uncommon for a group of two or three inside such a hut to be suddenly startled by an explosion in the fireplace. Some devilish fellow had dropped a handful of cartridges down the chimney.

At a meeting Feb. 9, 1864 the Regt. passed a resolution that "We will never lay down our arms till our independence is recognized." Other regiments did the same. I was 21 years old on that date.

In late winter we had issued to us day after day without change, a ration of corn meal. We ate corn so much that our teeth staid on edge; even freshly cooked, the bread would taste sour. When spring came on we were helped out by finding growing plentifully in the fields a wild plant called "cress," which boiled with bacon was very nice if young and tender. The poke weed too, when quite young, made good greens. During the winter, aside from the corn bread, the great stand-by was "Hoppin' John"—rice and cowpeas boiled together.

I will quote a few passages from my diary: "Sunday, Feb. 28, 1864—In the afternoon we hear that the enemy is advancing, and that Genl. Stuart has ordered away all citizens living between the Rapidan and the Robinson. . . . Feb. 29th Regt. is mustered. Immediately after being mustered, we (left wing) go on picket relieving Orr's Rifles. Co. H to Walker's Ford. About noon we hear firing up the river, which continues 2 or 3 hours. . . . March 2nd. Hear that the enemy's cavalry is between us and some of our Infantry on the opposite side of the river, and that there has been some fighting near Madison C. H. . . . March 5th. Hear the enemy is crossing the river below, advancing their whole force. . . . March 14th. A corps of Sharpshooters being planned, our Regt. is ordered to detail 2 non-commissioned officers and 20 men, of which our Co. is to furnish one non-commissioned officer and one private."

☆ 4 ☆

A Scout and Sharpshooter

ATTACHED TO A SHARPSHOOTING BATTALION — SCOUTING BEYOND
THE RAPIDAN — THE PLANK ROAD — THE WILDERNESS AGAIN
— ENTRENCHED AT SPOTSYLVANIA — THE COLONEL'S MARE —
"BLOODY ANGLE" — SCOUTING MISSIONS — CAPTURED

☆ ☆ ☆ ☆ ☆ ☆ ☆ ☆ ☆ ☆ ☆

BLACKWOOD and I had made up our minds to get into the
Sharpshooters' Corps upon its reorganization for the next
summer's campaign if possible. So we now applied to Capt.
Barnwell to let us go. But a difficulty arose; he was willing
to let one of us go, but not both. I was a sergeant and Blackwood a lance corporal, and the captain said he could not
spare two non-commissioned officers. Besides, the detail called
for one non-commissioned officer and one private.

Blackwood offered to let me go, he remaining with the
company. But since he had been a Sharpshooter the summer
before, while I was at home getting well of my wound, I
considered the place his by right. Then Blackwood proposed
that the captain let me go as the Non. Com., he going as a
private. Seeing us both so eager, Capt. Barnwell at last consented to this arrangement. I am glad to say that very soon
Blackwood was given his place as a Non. Com. officer in
the Corps. The Battalion was three companies, A, B, & C,
and I think numbered about 50 men each. Our company, A,
was under command of Lieut. Hasell of Charleston; the
Battalion was under command of Capt. Wm. Simpson Dunlop,
of the 12th Regt.

On March 17th I obtained permission to forage on the

other side of the Rapidan. Crossing early in the morning, I went as far as the Robinson River. I returned with two cabbages given me by a lady, who gave me also a mug of milk and some bread and butter. At her house, I looked thro' a spyglass, and saw the enemy's pickets and a signal flag waving.

This expedition I made, not so much to forage, as to spy out the land. I had got so weary of inaction that I determined upon no longer awaiting the turn of events, but going more than half way to meet them. With a pass to shield me from arrest by our cavalry, I plodded across the country to the Robinson River (5 miles). I visited a cavalry post, from whom I got some little information as to the lay of the land; and from the dwelling near by I viewed the enemy's country through a glass. Beyond the Robinson River lay a broad open field, gradually rising from the river, and on top of the hill was stationed the enemy's picket. I returned to camp revolving the situation in my mind.

I think it was the next day, just about sundown, that I crossed the Rapidan at a narrow, unguarded ford, having neither permission nor pass. It was soon quite dark, so that traveling through the fields, I was often near losing my way, having traveled it previously only once. But at length I found myself on high ground overlooking the river. It had turned bitterly cold, and for a moment I was tempted to abandon the enterprise, rather than attempt so cold a passage, at night, of a stream whose depth I did not know. But deciding that it would be inglorious for a Sharpshooter to postpone a scouting expedition for a mere matter of cold, I was soon standing naked on the banks of the Robinson, for I decided it would be more prudent to try the stream first unencumbered with clothes and gun.

Entering the water, I found it icy cold. I went on—knee deep—hip deep—breast deep, battling the swift current, which came just under my chin as I touched the opposite bank. Struggling back, half frozen, I realized that it would be foolish to try to transport gun and clothes across when I had just barely made it without them. Disappointed and ashamed, I drew on my clothes and started back.

After blundering along in the darkness for about two miles, I came to a little frame house standing alone and deserted at the edge of a wood—probably a country school house. I opened the door, looked in, and entered. Striking a match, I saw the one room, bare and empty, but with a big fireplace that caught my fancy. I gathered a little dry wood, built a small fire, and sat down to warm myself. Soon I stretched out before the fire, and before I knew it, I was asleep. Much later, I awoke, rose, and went to the door. Far and wide the ground lay white with snow, while the flakes kept falling thick and fast. Deciding to wait until the storm slackened, I replenished the fire, lay down again and dozed.

Near dawn, I looked out again. Still the snow fell. Deciding to wait no longer, I strode out and resumed my dejected retreat. Crossing some little brooks, I saw they were muddy and somewhat swollen. But this did not prepare me for the sight that met my eyes when I drew up at the Rapidan River. At the little ford where I had crossed the evening before, the water catching me at the hips, was now a swollen, muddy, rushing torrent, far over my head in depth—a flood of melted snow. Leaning on my rifle, I viewed the scene with desperation. Was I to enter that icy water, amidst this driving snow storm and swim it? There was but one alternative—to walk up-stream eight miles to Liberty Mills, where there was a bridge—and a picket. Having no pass, I would be arrested and taken to the camp and punished. Me, a non-commissioned officer, and a Sharpshooter!

The next minute my jacket was lying on the snow. Naked and with my rifle held high in my left hand, I entered the water, which caught me above the breast. A minute more and I was battling the current with my right hand, the rifle still aloft in the left. Landing a good way below, I pulled myself out and walked upstream, feeling as though thousands of needles pierced my body in every part. Laying my gun on the ground, I re-entered the water, swimming now with both hands. I did my clothes into two bundles, and with one of them in my left hand, again I made the passage, and again returned for the last bundle. By the time I had completed this last journey, my hands and arms were so numb with cold, that I could not get into my clothes. My nerveless arms dropped to my side, and my fingers could grasp nothing. In anguish, I looked around for help.

Across a field was a dwelling. My feet feebly obeying my will, I started toward it. A negro man in the back yard of the house saw me, and came toward me. He helped me into the kitchen, called the master of the house, and returned for my things. Wrapped in blankets, I was placed in a chair before the fire, and wood was piled on. And there I sat drawn close to a roaring fire, my feet in a tub of hot water with pepper in it, drinking red pepper tea. And thus ingloriously ended my scout to the Robinson.

It was within the next three weeks that Zack, our cousin, joined us, we taking him into our mess. He was just sixteen, and life seemed just opening up before him. None could foresee the tragic end.

On the 6th of April, the Battalion of Sharpshooters was officially organized, and inspection held. After that we used to practice shooting at a target. We practiced judging distances also, for it is essential to a soldier to know how far his enemy is from him, in order to adjust his sights properly.

And so the spring of 1864 drew on. We were awakened in the morning by the reveille, and at the tap of a drum we formed the ranks and went out to drill and dress parade, and the tattoo sang us to sleep. But one day, May 4, 1864, the long roll beat for a deeper purpose, and falling in, we marched away from our log cabins forever.

On Wednesday, the 4th of May, 1864, there was preaching at the chapel, and many of us were there. Suddenly the preacher paused. Through the camps the long roll was sounding, calling the men to arms. A short benediction, and we sped to quarters, to find the camp under orders to cook at once and march. But we were given no time to cook.

"Fall in, men, fall in," and away slid the rattling, shuffling, close-jointed column, through camp after camp deserted, out into the high road, through Orange Court House, and beyond. As we passed through the town, I bought a little box of biscuits and cakes and gave it to Zack, our new recruit. Continuing our march down the Plank Road, we bivouacked that night in the woods, near Verdier's Mill.

Thursday, May 5th, we continued our march down the Plank Road, after a while coming across traces of cavalry fighting—dead men and horses. In places, the woods were on fire. Farther down the Plank Road, the Brigade formed line-of-battle. The Sharpshooters were thrown in front, and we advanced. Suddenly we struck the enemy in the Wilderness and were checked. After a few minutes' fighting, the Brigade was at our backs. The Sharpshooters were condensed on the right, in line-of-battle, the right of the Battalion resting on the Plank Road. A fearful fire of musketry from the enemy swept the woods, and many were killed and wounded. Our line was ordered to lie down.

From my position on the edge of the road (which ran perpendicular to our line and to the enemy's, crossing both) I had a clear view forward for perhaps a third of a mile. But the forest was too dense to see much of the enemy, who, like ourselves kept out of the road.

Some few hundred yards down the road on the edge of the woods was an abandoned caisson or cannon. A man stepped to it, and sheltered behind it, fired his rifle, the bullet just missing me lying in the ditch. I returned the shot. Four or five times he fired at me, barely missing me, I firing in return. Finally a shot grazed the back of my shoulder, striking the wooden bar across my knapsack, indenting it deeply.

The battle raged heavily, not only in our midst, but to right and left, especially to the right on the other side of the Plank Road. Suddenly the battle grew more furious on the right; there were cheers from the enemy, and here came our men in retreat, moving obliquely toward us. Then the enemy advanced heavily in our front, our line gave way, and in two minutes the Plank Road was jammed with a disorderly, flying mass of Confederates, calling to one another by name and regiment, "Rally! Rally! Rally!" while the enemy continued to press forward, sending bullets in showers. It was a rout for the time.

In this disorganized crowd of men moving in all directions except toward the front, the Sharpshooters too had become scattered. Seeing one or two, I called to them, telling them to stay close by me and keep watch for others. Soon we had collected eight men. Breaking off twigs of pine, we set the green bunches in our hats to help us to hang together, about faced, and marched back obliquely toward the right, where we heard heavy firing still going on and where we knew the Confederates were still fighting. How up to this time we had escaped whole seemed almost miraculous.

Pressing on through the forest, we passed over a line-of-battle which lay behind a low earthwork, a ten minutes' construction, and pushed on to the front. As we ran forward, we passed General Lane, who sat on horseback a little in rear of his Brigade. Seeing us and supposing we were of the detail who kept the line supplied with ammunition from the wagons at the rear, he called to us, "Are you bringing in cartridges?"

"Yes, in our cartridge boxes!" we answered, holding them up and shaking them at him.

"That's right," he said.

The next minute we were fighting, side by side, amongst Lane's North Carolinians, in a dense wood, without undergrowth. So dense, that although we fought at close quarters, men falling thick and fast all about, we could only now and then see one or two as they flitted here and there. The roar of the rifles was incessant and the woods were half-dim with smoke, while a strong smell of sulphur pervaded the air. Directly Duncan Leach of Co. E. was wounded, and soon after, Eldred Rhodes of Co. G., both of 1st Regt. There were now left but six of us.

The fight continued, neither side making a charge, as it ought to have done. Either side by a charge could have driven its enemy. Once our line was near giving way, but the exertions of some of the officers saved it. As dusk drew on, fire could be seen streaming from the guns. Still, for an hour into the night, fought these two lines of men a bloody fight, firing at the flash of one another's guns.

When finally it was over, I marched back with my five men to the Plank Road, to find the Brigade if possible, carrying a statement given me by a North Carolina officer that we had fought in his command, so no fault could be found with us for being absent from our own. At the Plank Road we fortunately came across Center, one of Gen. McGowan's couriers, who told us where to find the Brigade. They were in line under arms on the other side of the Plank Road, holding about the same position they had held in the morning before the enemy advanced. In the darkness, my companions and I scattered, each seeking his own company in the Regt. Our line was lying down, keeping awake, expecting to be attacked, for the enemy were only a stone's throw in front. Both sides had pickets out, and there were no fires. Maybe there was some little gap in our line between regiments; I found myself alone, uncertain of direction, nobody in sight in the darkness. Fearful lest I walk into the enemy lines, I stopped, then called out, "First South Carolina?"

A voice nearby answered, "Here! This way!"

Another voice, also nearby, but in an opposite direction, said, "Don't go that way; that's a Yankee."

I stopped and kept still a moment. Then deciding the last speaker sounded more like a Confederate, I cocked my rifle and walked toward him. I don't remember just how I satisfied myself that this judgment was correct, before going up to him; but I presume it was by inquiring as to his regiment and commanding officers. But soon I was in the line again, and with my company.

Then I learned that Zack had been shot through both knees. He died of his wounds about the 4th of August, having been mortally wounded in his first battle.

At daybreak, May 6, 1864, the Battalion took up a position

behind a low range of breastworks, the Sharpshooters being deployed about 200 yards in advance. I was on the right of the line (my customary post as 1st Sergt. of Co. A.). In a little while, the man nearest me called softly, beckoning to me. As I stooped beside him, he pointed toward the front, saying, "Look there!"

When I could see nothing in particular, he said, "Don't you see? It's the Yankee line-of-battle!"

Sure enough, in their blue clothes scarcely distinguishable from the green of the forest in the dim light, were the enemy, slowly moving by the flank, evidently preparing to advance. Ordering the men not to fire, thus precipitating the attack, I hurried to Capt. Dunlop, who sent me on the run to Gen. McGowan, now commander of the Brigade. Hurrying back, I had just taken my position on the right again, when the advance of the enemy opened the fight.

Though only a line of skirmishers against a line of battle, we fought stubbornly, dropping back slowly, to give the line-of-battle behind us good time to meet the enemy with a full volley. As we reached the earthwork, dropping behind it into the line, what was our surprise and shame to see our line-of-battle rise and flee the enemy, scarcely firing a shot! The men, doubtless, were still under the influence of the terrible encounter along the Plank Road of the evening previous, and they ran like deer through the wood, leaving the enemy far behind. Down a slope we went, across a brook, up the field on the other side, halting only when General Lee rode up to us exclaiming, "I am surprised to see such a gallant brigade running like a flock of geese!"

No troops in the world could have stood *that!* The halt was immediate and decisive. The enemy then appeared across the field at the edge of the wood we had just quitted, but a few well-directed shots of artillery drove them back. We moved forward through the woods and halted at a rail fence, which we tore down and piled as a defense in case of being attacked, posting videttes in front. Directly the vidette on the right reported the enemy advancing, then another vidette fired and ran in. With rifles cocked, we awaited the advance of the enemy. But they did not come. I went down to the left and questioned Plaxico, the vidette who had fired. He told me that not only had he seen one of the enemy, but had killed him.

Everything still remaining quiet, I passed the word along the line that I was going out to reconnoitre, and not to fire upon me when I returned. Moving cautiously, I came to a little open space where on a bare spot of red clay, lay the dead man sure enough. He was lying on his face, his gun under him. He had on boots, and a ring on his finger. These some of our men afterwards took. This was a species of demoralization which grew to be too common. It was practiced on both sides, but was no doubt more common on the Confederate side than on the Federal, for two reasons. First, the needs of the Confederates were greater, they themselves seldom possessing anything worth taking. Secondly, in those campaigns in which I was engaged, we whipped nearly all the fights, seldom leaving a field of battle in the hands of the Union army, to be plundered. I do not think there was much robbing of the dead in the beginning of the war. But as time went on and the men became hardened, and their necessities greater, the pillage of the fields extended not only to the taking of articles of value, such as money, watches, and rings, but even to coats and trousers. Blackwood says that he has seen dead men stripped entirely naked, but this I am sure I have never seen.

Sat. May 7, '64, we moved a little to the right into the Wilderness. In the afternoon we continued the march to the right down the line of breastworks, and marched some that night. Thus began that sliding movement of the armies, the enemy continually endeavoring to outflank us on the right, and always finding himself opposed by Lee. This movement ended in placing Grant before Richmond on the James with fearful losses in killed and wounded, when he might have attained the same position without any loss by ascending the James. Hardly ever, until reaching Spottsylvania Court House, were we in fields—always the Wilderness.

While waiting stationary behind the breastworks, not knowing when the enemy might attack, all at once we heard cheering far on the right, so far that it was almost inaudible through faintness. Gradually it grew louder and louder, nearer and nearer, until we knew that it was a cheer which, started on the right of the army, was passing down to the left, taken up in succession by the troops as it approached. Nearer, nearer, and now it was just on our right hand, and we took it up. As we quieted, we heard it passing on to the left, gradually dying out. But it had hardly passed us when we heard another cheer coming from the right. It slips down and down till we take that up in turn, only to hear a third on its way, and so on till ten cheers had passed like waves, the length of the army. I think there were generally three cheers in motion on the line at one time. I suppose one must be a soldier to feel the full charm of such cheering. Heard at first faintly, in the far distance, it comes like the breath of a wind, drawing nearer and nearer, till it reaches you with a blast as of trumpets.

Since then I have often heard this extended cheering, but never since so well executed nor with such sublime effect as that night in the Wilderness. After the ten cheers had all passed, came a message, started and forwarded the same way. We could not distinguish the words till close to us. Then we heard, "Grant's wounded! Grant's wounded!" and so we passed it on. But just to our left they got it wrong, and (omitting the syllable before the last) the message went on its way "Grant's dead! Grant's dead!" So the right of the army had it that Grant was wounded, the left that he was dead.

This method of transmitting messages came to be put to practical use. For instance, the message might be conveyed a mile or two very rapidly, "Tell Major _____ that General _____ wants to see him at once at the Dabney house."

At daylight May 8th I went scouting out front to try to ascertain the whereabouts of the enemy. After a while, I returned to the line, having discovered nothing. Then we heard a wild turkey gobbling somewhere out front. Lt. Hasell gave permission for Hawthorne and me to go out and try to kill it for food. We proceeded very cautiously, but the farther we went, the farther seemed the turkey. After a while we came to a narrow valley, thro' which ran a small stream. On the opposite side were hills covered with forest. We slipped cautiously down through low pine bushes to the stream, where we found a great many footprints, which we judged to be those of the enemy.

Directly we heard a noise in the woods opposite as of troops marching thro' the dry leaves, and I caught the gleam of a gun barrel in the woods. Moving cautiously forward, from one tree to another, we got close enough to discover that they were Confederates, a line of skirmishers. We joined them for a while, but soon left them to explore an opposite direction, and Hawthorne and I came upon a breastwork, deserted but strewn with all kinds of soldier's equipments from boiled beef to Adams' Arithmetic. I speak by the card, for I recognized the old school book as it lay there on the ground. Not caring to push our advance farther, we filled our haversacks with hard tack and beef, and returned quickly to the boys. We distributed the provender in lieu of the turkey which we had not been able to get, and reported to Capt. Dunlop.

I had just sat down to eat a piece of the beef which one of the boys had broiled for me, when a message came from Genl. McGowan that Maj. Genl. Wilcox, commanding the Division, wished to see me immediately. After questioning me closely as to the situation in front, Genl. Wilcox ordered that the Sharpshooters should move forward and give a loud cheer upon reaching the breastwork. This was done. Marching still beyond, we found in a field a great number of knapsacks piled up, besides blankets, oilcloths, tentflies etc. strewn all thro' the field and woods. I never saw a field so rich in plunder. It looked as though the enemy had fled in dismay, leaving all their property. No enemy in sight, we proceeded to help ourselves.

Continuing the sliding movement to the right, we took

position about midday, May 9th, at Spottsylvania Court House, a place of only a few houses, and entrenched. The Sharpshooters were thrown out in front in a wood. There were logs lying about and these we took to make rifle pits. From the general method of constructing protection for sharpshooters by digging a hole in the ground and throwing the earth up in front of it as a breastwork, arose the use of the word "pits" as applied to any construction serving the same purpose. A pile of rails was called a "rifle pit," and so with the logs. No hole was dug; the rails were simply arranged in low piles behind which the men lay.

After a little, we moved forward thro' the woods and crossed a brook. Then, ascending a hill thro' a dense pine thicket, we halted, being now a mile or more from the line-of-battle. Leaving the men here, I took Oscar Bookman and went in front, trying to find out just where the enemy lay. About 50 yards ahead we found a road upon which we turned left. Soon we came to a large field lying on our right, a big house in the field. There the enemy were entrenching. We then returned and reported.

This day Ben Powell came in from sharpshooting and told us he had killed (or wounded) a Yankee officer. He had fired at long range at a group of horsemen whom he recognized as officers. At his shot, one fell from his horse, and the others dismounted and bore him away. That night the enemy's pickets called over to ours that Major General Sedgwick, commanding the 6th corps, was killed that day by a sharp-shooter.

Later that day we threw out videttes in our front upon the road Bookman and I had scouted. I went again to the road, taking to the right, instead of the left as before. Near an old broken gateway, our rightmost vidette post, I climbed a tree to reconnoitre. I could see the enemy's picket line in a field beyond the pines. A fire broke out in the field, and I saw the Yankee pickets collect and beat it out with brush. Some of the boys brought me a spyglass belonging to an officer of Thomas's (Ga.) Brigade Sharpshooters, connecting on our right.

I came down and proceeded farther to the front, along a rail fence which ran perpendicular to the road. After going about 70 yards, I came to where a crossfence abutted against my fence, separating the pine thicket which lay on my left from an open field occupied by the enemy. I crossed my fence, and on hands and knees crept down alongside the other fence getting closer to the enemy, who were soon in plain sight. Not daring to expose myself by climbing this fence, I lay flat on the ground and by exerting all my strength, I lifted the panel of fence at a corner, enough to slip the end of a rail out sideways. This allowed two rails in the same panel to rest one on the other. Another rail moved in the same way left a gap close to the ground, three rails wide. Through this I crawled, and screening myself behind some bushes about waist high, I got quite close to the enemy's line.

They were busy fortifying. There was a house there (Beverly House probably) and here they had turned their works back to protect their left flank, we being then on the right of our army. Having examined the position attentively, I returned to the line and reported, and sent Silas Ruff to the corner of the fence to keep watch.

Then I took Bookman again and explored the road still farther to the right, till we came to a stream, which I suppose was the river. On the other side of the stream was a large open field, in the midst of which sat a large house (Anderson House probably). Here was a picket post of the enemy's cavalry, and midway between the post and the river was a vidette sitting on his horse in the open field. It was a tempting shot for Ben. But not wishing to raise an alarm, we returned to the Sharpshooters and reported.

Tuesday, May 10th, the Sharpshooters were relieved from duty in the morning. Having nothing to do, I went down across a field where Ben Powell, with his Whitworth rifle was sharpshooting. Ben was not attached to the Battalion, being independent in his movements. There had been a number of Whitworth rifles (with telescope sight) brought from England, running the blockade. These guns with ammunition had been distributed to the army, our brigade receiving one. It was given to Powell, as he was known to be an excellent shot. In campaigns he posted himself wherever he pleased, for the purpose of picking off the enemy's men.

I shot the gun a few times. It kicked powerfully. Blackwood says that once at Petersburg Powell gave him the gun to shoot, and as there was nobody particular in sight to shoot at, he held it up at a high angle and fired it over into the besiegers' camp. Not long after, in a Northern paper, he read an account of two men being shot at a well, struck by the same ball, which had come so far that the report of the gun was not heard. And the day given was the same day he fired the Whitworth. Blackwood always inclined to add that two and two together.

Wed. May 11, about noon, I asked permission of General Wilcox to go scouting. Saying that he would be glad to have me go, he instructed me to get if possible in rear of the enemy's left, which then rested opposite us, and ascertain how many lines of breastworks guarded their flank, and how strongly manned. So, with Ben Powell as a companion, I started from the Court House, on the road leading by Massaponax Church. We passed through our infantry pickets and went to one or two farm houses, where we obtained the loan of spyglasses, and where from the upper windows we observed the position of the enemy and chose a route. We also got advice as to the most direct way to a bridge we would have to cross.

As we cut through woods and fields to reach the bridge, a rabbit jumped up, and I shot it. Just before we reached the bridge, a heavy storm came up, and we took shelter under it. When the storm had passed, we concealed our rabbit under the bridge and proceeded. While toiling along the wet, muddy road about half a mile past the bridge, we saw a horseman coming. Not knowing his stripe, we hid in a fence corner till he came up, when seeing he wore a blue overcoat, we ordered him to halt. Showing us his grey trousers, he convinced us that he was a Confederate, and told us our cavalry were picketed a little farther ahead. On reaching our picket, we could see the enemy's cavalry picket at the house (Anderson House) where Bookman and I had seen them on the 9th, but now from a different direction.

Moving farther outward, we followed a road which led in a direction paralleling the lines, and toward the enemy's left. After a little, we thought it wiser to quit the main road, taking a small road branching on the right hand, that appeared to be seldom used. We soon came to a field and in it a farmhouse. Approaching the farm house, we introduced ourselves to the elderly gentleman, Mr. Hart, who met us, as Confederate soldiers seeking information as to the country round about. But, though we were answered politely enough, the replies actually gave no information. We were asked from what state we came, and when I said I was from Augusta, Ga., Miss Emma Hart, who had been lending her wits to assist her father in giving his vague replies, reeled off a list of Augusta people, some of whom I knew, some not. When she asked, "Do you know Marion Stovall?" I described him so accurately that the young lady called to someone inside to come out, "And give these gentlemen all the information they want; they are Southerners." Being very close to the main road from Spottsylvania to Fredericksburg and quite near the enemies' lines, the Harts had been cautious, lest we prove to be Yankee spies.

With a better picture in mind of the lay of the land, we left the Harts' and took to the woods, our feet making little noise on the rain-dampened leaves. It was now about sunset. Presently we came to the edge of the woods, and saw before us an orchard. Skirting along the edge of the orchard we heard in front a sound like the marching of troops through woods. We stopped and listened, soon hearing them halt, commence chopping wood, and calling to one another. We passed through a thicket and came out into an open field, on top of a low hill. On top of another hill, a little hollow lying betwixt us, I could faintly discern the outlines of two men with rifles on their shoulders, apparently coming in our direction. Powell and I ran to a fence some half a dozen yards from us, climbed over it, and squatted in a corner, intending to let the men pass and then proceed. After we had waited some time, no one coming, we began cautiously to descend the hill, keeping close to the fence.

We had gone only a little distance when we heard talking in the hollow below us. Concealing ourselves amongst the low hanging boughs of a cedar, we waited, listening. It was now quite dark. The talking continued, and soon a number of lights sprang up, and then we saw many men clustering around the fires, stretching their fly tents and preparing supper. We could distinguish some of their words. We heard a man say, "They told us a d-d lie about Butler taking Richmond."

We were now about 40 yards from the enemy. After remaining here a while, learning nothing except the name of the Regt., we pressed on, moving toward the enemy's right, until the whole camp appeared to lie to our right in a field. Posting Powell in a secure place in a fence corner, instructing him to return and report what so far we had found out, in case I was not back in reasonable time, I left, after agreeing with him on a signal (loud snapping of fingers) when I returned. I went out into the field, rifle in hand, and passed between the enemy videttes unobserved.

Having crossed a little stream a yard wide, I stole up thro' some low pine bushes a little way, when just in front I saw a fly tent pitched. Just then a man rode up on horseback and began talking with someone in the tent, addressing him as Colonel. I overheard a good deal of what was said, the Colonel ordering the disposition of the regiments of the brigade. Then the horseman rode away. I crept around and approached a house a little farther on. Leaning on the yard fence, I looked at the cannons, the horses, and the men in the yard. Hailing the men, I asked what artillery this was, and they told me.

I then went farther, and asked some questions of some men I saw in the field standing around a camp fire, I taking great care to keep well back out of the light lest they see my grey clothes. I went still farther, reaching what I judged to be the enemy's extreme left, without once seeing breastworks. So it now appearing that there were *no* breastworks protecting the enemy's left, the information I had been sent out to get, and furthermore, since I had learned whose was the command, and that they had just occupied it, I thought it time to go back and report—if I could get back. For it was but good fortune that so far no one had said, "Who are you? Come here to the light." I was inside the enemy lines, his campfires dotting the field, my only protection the darkness of the night.

Back I started, the same way I had come, stopping at the yard fence a moment to covet one of the fine horses, stepping along boldly, avoiding the appearance of stealth. Just as I neared the Colonel's little tent, I saw someone on horseback again talking to the Colonel, and I had to circle around a pine bush to escape being seen by him as he rode away. I was close to the tent, and there about twenty feet in front of the tent stood a horse.

I saw nobody. But inside the tent the Colonel was awake; I had just heard him talking. There was no door or flap; the entrance was wide open. But a bold attempt might capture the Colonel's horse. But what if I were discovered? Then it would take only a dash through the picket line, whose positions I knew. On this black night not too risky.

I walked softly toward the tent, keeping the horse between me and the entrance. I reached the animal, which stood quite still. I put up my hand and felt the leather halter, tied in a knot. Not taking time to untie, I took out my knife and cut the halter close to the tree. Then I moved slowly off, the horse making little noise in following. Having gained a little distance, I increased my pace, reached the little stream, and jumped it, my capture following. We passed out between the videttes undiscovered, and hurried to the spot where I had left Powell. A snap or two of the fingers and he answered. He had been on the point of moving off to report, thinking I must have been captured.

We hurried thro' the woods, came to a little road, where Powell, on my invitation, mounted, and after a time came into the big road that we had traveled just after leaving our cavalry picket, and soon reached the picket. There by the light of the fire we got our first good view of the capture. It was a fine black mare, with a colonel's saddle cloth on her back. The cavalry admired her very much, pronouncing her a fine acquisition for the Confederacy.

We retrieved our rabbit from under the bridge, and just at daylight reached the line, tired, wet, hungry, and sleepy. I asked where I could find Genl. Wilcox, but nobody could tell me. Finally I lay down by the fire, almost worn out, asking the boys to wake me in ten minutes. But I had hardly lain down when the order came, "Fall in! Fall in!"

We were hurried rapidly to the left, then turned toward the front. A heavy fire of musketry was going on, and bullets began to fall thick as we went forward. Directly we were running by the flank along a breastwork down which the bullets were streaming, men falling all round us. There was not much order, only a great crowd of soldiers, in column, rushing into battle.

We had learned that the enemy had surprised and taken part of our breastworks and we must retake them. They were in a position that enfiladed our line and the rear of the breastworks, and the bullets were coming down the breastwork, but rather from the rear. The Sharpshooters became scattered. I found myself with a few men of Co. H and with Major Alston. As our men continued to get upon the scene of action, which was in narrow compass, the roar of musketry grew louder and louder, with increasing numbers. The breastworks were crowded with Confederates all mixed up, but fighting like demons.

How describe this terrific battle, the bloodiest, the hardest fought, the most obstinate of the war, for the ground covered? The enemy had at dawn surprised Johnson's Division in the breastwork, and now held the works for a considerable length. Our men, pouring along this same breastwork, came to where the enemy held it, so that the enemy's right and our right overlapped, only the breastwork between them. I did not reach this point, which was the most deadly and the hardest fought. But outside the breastworks stood and lay the enemy also, in great force, flags crowded together. The firing was incessant, punctuated by brief lulls during which each side urged the other to surrender.

Once a small party of Confederates, being subjected to a fierce cross fire, raised a white flag. Immediately the cry arose from our ranks, "Shoot them fellows! Shoot them fellows!" and it was jerked down. But the enemy, seeing the flag, ceased firing and raised a flag of truce. An officer came forward saying the surrender would be accepted. But he was told that it was no surrender, that the white flag (a handkerchief) had been raised without authority.

There was no artillery. There may have been a little in the beginning, but there was none now. Artillery could not live in such a close, hand-to-hand fight. Branches of trees were falling, shot off by rifle balls. A tree 20 inches in diameter fell, cut down by rifle balls. The stump of it is now in Washington in the National Museum. Some were severely wounded by these falling limbs, Rothwell ("Promptly") of Co. H. being one. 1st Sergt. Mackey had been killed. Capt. Barnwell was wounded. Lieut. Miller was wounded. Lt. Col. Shooter was killed. His brother, Lt. Shooter, was killed. Col. McCreary was wounded. Capt. Brailsford, Capt. Kelley, Lieut. Armstrong, were wounded. Sergt. Force who, wounded at Chancellorsville, had been with me in Manchester Hospital, was killed.

Where the lines overlapped, the men said they and the enemy both mostly fired without showing their heads above the works. Guns were loaded, held up to the breastwork, depressed, and the trigger pulled with the thumb. One man— I think it was Owens of Co. H—told me he several times took in his hand the barrel of a gun pointing down on him, held it up till it was fired, then let it go. But there were some men who *would* stand up—stand up calling for loaded guns, which were passed to them. They would fire a few shots and fall, shot through the head. It was Owens with two or three others who at one time occupied a small detached mound—"Cannon-pit" Owens called it. Fortified and a little elevated, it gave a better command of the field. They had a whole box of ammunition, and from this point they kept up a continuous fire. By some means they took a prisoner. Him they compelled to load guns or pass cartridges—I forget now which Owens said. But that was wrong.

Lying behind the breastwork, without food for so long, worn out from two days and nights without rest or sleep, I did an incredible thing—I fell asleep. Just when, I don't know; but fall asleep I did, and I suppose I was taken for dead, for nobody waked me. Some time in the night I was awakened by the tramp of a large body of men rushing past me.

I jumped up and asked, "What troops are these?"

"Louisiana Battalion."

A dead man lay by my side. The firing, though not altogether over, was much weaker, and I soon learned that the Confederate line was under order to retire from the position, a few at a time, and take up a position at an inner line of works, which, I believe, had been built thro' the day. Going out in the dark, I fell into a ditch, an entrenchment, I suppose. I came down with my whole weight on somebody who gave a fearful groan, but whether he was a wounded man, I don't know.

This description can give but the faintest idea of that terrible battle of Spottsylvania, "Bloody Angle," or Horse Shoe Bend as it is also called. About daylight the Regt. began to gather together, the different groups of men, and to organize as well as possible. Everybody seemed fagged out, and I don't think there is one but will say with me that he hopes never to have such a fight again.

Having no diary of this time, I find that the movements and succession of events of the next few days are obscure and almost forgotten. But we hung around Spottsylvania, doing not much fighting, I think—perhaps only skirmishing. I remember Powell coming up one day with a hole in his hat. He had been dueling with one of the enemy's sharpshooters who proved himself so excellent a shot, that Powell thought it prudent to retire.

I think it was Sunday, May 15th, that I went over to the field of battle, which the enemy declined to occupy. Dead bodies, most of them enemies', thickly strewed the ground, swollen to twice the size of men. The air was horribly foul with the stench of decaying bodies. In some places they lay so thick on the gound that I had to pick my way amongst them. And to shun the fearful gaze of their open eyes, I held my head up, looking ahead, afraid to look down. Nearly all our men had been buried. I saw the grave of Lt. Col. and Lt. Shooter, two brothers, buried together.

The breastwork where our men had fought had been built in crescent shape, with traverses inside. The traverses were invaluable to our line, suffering from flank fire. Without them the line would have been untenable. The throwing up so much breastwork had made great pits between the traverses. There having been rain, these pits were now pools of water, so saturated with powder as to be nearly black as ink. In this black water and on the ground outside, lay rifles—broken and unbroken—cartridge-boxes, cap boxes, belts, knapsacks, canteens, haversacks, cartridges, ammunition boxes, clothing of all kinds, blankets, oilcloths, tentcloths, bayonets, ramrods—torn, broken, bent, scarred, black, and bloody—a very hell. I said to myself at the time if a man wants to see hell upon earth, let him come and look into this black, bloody hole—upon this horrid confusion, these wet, muddy graves— this reeking mass of corruption of rotting corpses, that fill the air with this intolerable stench. How a man can look upon such a scene and still take pleasure in war seems past belief. Yet the revulsion of feeling is only temporary. In a few days, I was "spoiling for a fight," and so were the rest.

I did not stay here long, for there was sharpshooting going on not far off, and now and then a bullet struck near me.

As I walked down the line, on my return, I saw a young Confederate soldier sitting on the breastwork, in an easy attitude. As I passed, I was on the point of saying something to him; in fact I had just cast my eyes upon his face, as one does when speaking to another, when I saw to my surprise and horror that he was stone dead. No doubt, he had been passed and repassed by our burial corps without notice, his posture deceiving them as it had me, into the supposition that he was alive.

My horse I turned over to Capt. R. E. B. Hewetson, our quartermaster, to ride, he taking my knapsack into one of his wagons, in return for the favor.

On the evening of May 16, 1864, the Brigade took position on the breastwork at Spottsylvania. A picket being put out, the Sharpshooters were allowed to sleep. Some pines had been felled and the boughs piled, and on these we spread our blankets, the ground being wet. Soon after falling asleep, I was awakened by the sound of talking. Capt. Dunlop was asking for volunteers to go scouting. I rose, offering my services.

"You are just the man I want," the Capt. said. "Take three men and report to Capt. Langdon Haskell (brother of our lamented Capt. William Haskell) at Brigade Headquarters."

Saying that two would do, I took Norton and Russell, who volunteered. At Headquarters, Capt. Haskell told us that General Lee suspected the enemy of being about to move on the Telegraph Road from Fredericksburg to Richmond. He had therefore ordered every Brigade Commander to learn what the enemy was doing in his immediate front.

I asked whether I should go directly out front or go around and try to get in the enemy's rear. He replied that I might do as I chose. Preferring the latter course, I fixed an hour next day by which I would return with information. Captain Haskell replied that I must be back—not next day— but within two hours!

I told him that it would be impossible, then, to circle around the enemy's lines; but that I doubted my ability to learn anything of consequence in front.

"If you can't get the information *outside* the lines, then you must go *inside*," Capt. Haskell replied.

Knowing that to penetrate the enemy lines directly in front and escape observation would be extremely difficult, I decided to draw as near as possible to their pickets and listen for the sound of troops moving. But here we heard nothing of any significance. So instructing my two men to keep 50 yards behind me, and whenever they heard me halted or talking to anybody, to wait a while, and if I did not return, to go back and report to Capt. Haskell, I proceeded toward the enemy picket line. I had got pretty close, and was hoping that amongst the pine bushes I might creep through unnoticed, when I had to cross a wet place, and my foot made a slight noise.

"Who comes there?" cried a sentinel.

"A friend," I answered.

"Come in, then," was the reply.

If by this time I had discovered anything worth reporting, I would have gone back. But having gained no information, it only remained to me to get inside, learn what I could, then attempt to escape. I walked quietly up to the pickets, the color of my uniform concealed by the darkness.

"What are you doing out there?" a sentinel demanded.

"I've been scouting down the Rebel lines."

"Where did you go out?"

"Lower down to the left; I belong to Hancock's corps."

Having posted myself from prisoners, I knew that corps was there, and could answer satisfactorily the questions as to division, brigade, and regiment, even naming some of the officers. I went on to say that I was making a short cut through the camp to report, instead of returning by the roundabout way I had come.

"Well, it may be all right," said the officer, "but I'll have to send you up to Brigade Headquarters."

"All right," I agreed casually.

Two men were detailed to go with me, but I was allowed to carry my own gun. Passing through a good deal of camp, my guards halted at the door of a large tent, and announced to the occupant that they had a man in custody who claimed to be a Federal scout.

From the darkened tent came a voice demanding, "What regiment do you belong to?"

"6th New York."

"You are a Southern soldier."

"You are altogether mistaken, sir."

"You are a Southern soldier. Come in here!"

I heard a match struck; a candle was lit. It was all up. I lifted the flap of the tent and stepped inside, rifle and all.

"Aha!" he said as he cast his eyes on me. "What state are you from?"

"South Carolina, sir."

"Aha!" He broke out in a laugh, and I followed suit.

He was Col. Sweitzer, commanding a brigade. He told me he had lived in the South and had known I was a Southerner, the first word I spoke. He talked right pleasantly with me for some time and asked me a good many general questions, amongst other things how our army fared for food. Luckily when I knew I was going out to scout, I had gone to our commissary, "Promptly," and inveigled from him a loaf of fresh-baked bread. This I handed to the colonel, inviting him to try it, saying we had plenty more like it. (Everything being fair in war, I hope that fib was pardonable.) He broke off a piece and ate it, pronouncing it excellent.

After a little more light, cheerful talk, the Colonel bade me a good night and a speedy exchange, for which I thanked him, intending to exchange myself before daylight if possible. Before I left, he ordered the guard to take my gun; but at my request allowed me to keep my belt, a very nice one which I had bought in South Carolina. Hanging to the belt was a short bowie knife, on the white handle of which was cut "Z. Benson." Zack had lent it to me at the opening of the campaign, and it was for the sake of the knife that I had asked to keep the belt.

As the guard conducted me through the camp, I continued

on the alert for any signs or sounds of movement, but discovered nothing. Arrived at a little cluster of tents, my guards delivered me over to a sergeant, asking of him a certificate. This he gave, writing with a pencil, by the light of a candle. I was now conducted to a cluster of fly tents on the edge of a pine thicket, beyond which heavier woods loomed up. Outside was a low fire by which sat a guard, rifle in hand. To him I was delivered.

I decided that my best plan was to pump this guard as to troop movements, if I could, then with any information I had gained, to make a run for the big woods, and trust to fortune for the rest. I thought the best way to draw him out would be to start bragging for my own side; this would set him bragging for his, and I hoped he would let some cats out of the bag. It worked to a charm. He told me a good deal, including a movement of the Corcoran Legion, and of heavy artillery men who had been manning the defenses of Washington being brought to the front, giving numbers, and more.

And now a thought struck me. Remembering that inside camp our men often kept guard with unloaded guns, I thought that if I could satisfy myself that his was unloaded, I could make the break with greater confidence. Leaning against a little pine just at my left hand was a rifle, belonging to another of the guards. If one of these guns was kept unloaded, all were apt to be. So I went on bragging on the prowess of our men, and presently I said, "Why, we can beat you at drilling—that's been proved. I don't claim to be one of our best, but I dare say I can go through the manual of arms better than you can."

With these words, I picked up the gun—he looking at me and saying little. Briskly obeying the commands as I gave them to myself, I came to the order, "Load in nine times—Load!" The gun passed to my left side; the butt dropped to the ground; my right hand went back as tho' to the cartridge box; I bit off the end of an imaginary cartridge; placed it in the muzzle; drew the ramrod; passed it down the barrel—the gun was empty! I replaced the ramrod; brought the gun to the right side; cocked it; drew a cap out of my vest pocket, and capped the gun. Setting the gun back against the tree, I asked, "There! Can you beat that?" And I just had it on my tongue to add, "Goodbye, old fellow," when the corporal of the guard appeared from nowhere, and posted another man in the old guard's place.

The new guard, a corporal, a tall well made fellow, leaned his gun against the tree right beside the one I had just placed there, and stood by the fire warming himself as the other two men walked away. Then, picking up a gun, he ordered me to come with him. We started off, he in front, along a line of wagons parked, the horses eating. Just beyond the wagons, ten yards or so to my right lay the edge of an oak woods, and I saw no tents in it. The corporal walked about a step in front of me, a little to my left, his rifle over his right shoulder. My left hand fell heavily on the gun barrel, which thudded to the ground, as I turned and sprang among the horses.

"Halt! Halt!" shouted the corporal. There was a second's silence, and then a cap snapped behind me.

"Stop that man! Stop that man!" I heard the corporal's voice as I darted amongst the trees, and I heard his feet, too, following close, as I struggled through the strip of woods; and he was not far behind when I broke into an open field where I was in full view. "Stop that man! Stop that man!" he continued to shout, hot at my heels as I pelted down a hill, jumped a ditch, and turned obliquely to the left heading for some pine woods. Running as I had never run before, I gained the woods a few paces ahead of my pursuer, but almost exhausted, when sharp upon my left came a party of armed men running, who caught me and held me fast.

A Prisoner of the Yankees

SUSPECTED OF SPYING — PRISONER OF WAR — ESCAPE FROM
POINT LOOKOUT PRISON — BAREFOOTED FUGITIVE — TAKEN FOR
A DESERTER — APPROACHING WASHINGTON — SWIMMING THE
POTOMAC — HOME TERRITORY BUT ENEMY HANDS — OLD
CAPITOL PRISON

☆ ☆ ☆ ☆ ☆ ☆ ☆ ☆ ☆ ☆ ☆

THE corporal came up and took charge of me, the whole
party accompanying me back to where they had me before.
On the way I suffered a great deal of abuse from the corporal,
who called me all kinds of villainous names, and when I dared
remonstrate, he spitefully thrust the point of his bayonet
into my leg—a hurt only temporary physical, but to my feelings
it lasted a long time. I appealed to the men, asking what
crime it was in a prisoner to attempt to escape, and one or
two took my part. Their expostulations had a good effect
upon the corporal's behavior; he cooled down to calling me
no worse names than "d--d rebel" and such.

Arrived back at the guard's quarters, the corporal said,
"I'll fix you so you won't run any more." Whereupon he got
out a small hempen rope, tied my hands behind my back, and
tied me to a tree. He had been cursing not only me, but the
gun also, for missing fire. He swore that it had never served
him such a trick before, and that I owed my life to its defec-
tion, as he had dead aim on me not ten steps off when he
pulled the trigger. Now when he came to the light he held up

the gun to look at it, and discovered that it was not his own. His own loaded gun leaned against the tree where he had placed it; he had taken instead the unloaded gun which I had capped.

I now realized the perilous position I was in. Having represented myself to the pickets as a Union scout, persisting in this assertion when brought before the commanding officer; having pumped the guard for information and then attempted to get away with it, I began to see that a strong case might be made against me as a spy. The talk that I overheard, such as, "The d--d spy! I thought it mighty strange his asking so many questions," added to my disquietude.

At length the compression of the ropes on my wrists became so painful that I asked if they would be so good as to change my position some way. Most of them paid no attention, but a sergeant came forward, and untying the ropes, tied me again, with my hands over my head, to a low limb. This relieved me for a time, but the new position soon began to be as painful. My hat, which had fallen off, was kindly placed on my head. My pockets were searched, and my purse containing only stamps and a little Confederate money was returned to me. But my diary was kept.

When day came (Tuesday, May 17, 1864) I was untied and taken to the Headquarters of Gen. Patrick, Provost Marshall—at the same house where on the night of May 11th, I had leaned against the fence looking at the artillery and the horses and talking to the Federal soldiers. Thence I was taken to Gen. Meade's Headquarters, at Anderson House, where Bookman and I had seen the cavalry picket on the 9th. An officer came out of the house and addressed me, opening his speech by accusing me of being a spy. I asked him what ground he had for making such a charge, which I denied.

For answer he produced my diary, asking, "Is this yours?"

"Yes, sir."

"Is this your writing?"

"It is, sir."

"Are you detached from your regular company?"

"Yes, sir."

"As what?"

"In a corps of Sharpshooters, sir."

"Are these Sharpshooters mounted?"

It flashed through my mind that I might somewhere have made mention of my captured mare in the book, and that he had read it. So I said, "Not as a general thing, sir. A few have horses that they use sometimes in scouting. I have one, now in charge of my Quartermaster."

Handing me a small strip of paper, he asked, "What were you doing with this in your book?"

I took it and read: "In the field, May 10, 1864—Received of Corporal Edward White, one Rebel Prisoner. (Signed) Thomas Black, Sgt. of Provost Guard."

(The names as here given are fictitious; I have forgotten the true ones).

I replied, "I never saw this paper before. It could not have been found in my book."

"But it *was* found in your book and sent me as part of your property."

"Colonel, there is some mistake here. You call me a rebel. How could I receive a rebel prisoner?"

"That's just what we don't understand," replied the Colonel. "*You* explain it."

Racking my brains, I suddenly remembered that the picket guard the night before had asked for and received a receipt for me, upon turning me over to the sergeant of the Provost Guard. This might well have been turned in along with my diary. When I offered this explanation to the Colonel, he took back the paper, scrutinized it and said, "Then how do you explain this discrepancy? You were captured last night, May 16th, and a receipt issued. But this paper is dated May 10th."

Peering at the paper extended in the Colonel's hand, I saw that this was so. But the zero was not fully joined and might conceivably have been intended for a 6.

Evidently not satisfied with this explanation, the Colonel continued his interrogation: "What were you doing when captured?"

"Scouting, sir."

"For what purpose?"

"I was ordered to learn whether you were moving, sir," I answered frankly, knowing that this admission could do no harm to the Confederacy.

"Then, upon being hailed, why did you claim to be a Union scout?"

"I hoped, sir, that they would not order me in, but would let me remain outside the picket lines."

"But upon being brought in you represented yourself to Colonel Sweitzer also as a Union scout."

"True, sir. But I had to be consistent. I hoped there was a chance *he* might let me go."

The Colonel stood thinking a moment. So far he had not mentioned my attempt to escape from the guard; and I never knew whether he was aware of it. Presently he continued, "Inside a Federal camp, you misrepresented yourself as a Union scout. Was not that spying?"

"Colonel," I protested, "I was taken *outside* your lines, armed with my regular arms, dressed in full grey uniform. Only the darkness of the night prevented my being recognized as a Confederate. Was it wrong to make use of this accidental advantage? Wouldn't your scouts have done the same thing?" Thus I argued with him for some time, and I think I was more eloquent than I ever have been before or since. He listened patiently, and seemed to feel interested.

Finally he told me that in all probability, I would be tried as a spy by court-martial in a few hours; but that I would not be condemned without a hearing. He added that he felt kindly toward me, would do all he could for me, and that he hoped I would come out safe. I thanked him, and he went back in the house.

That I now felt a good deal of alarm, I cannot deny. A trial by drum-head court-martial is a terrible ordeal. I realized that the case against me would be aggravated by certain suspicious circumstances which were likely to be brought out. The question about horses had aroused a fear that there were clues connecting me with the capture of the Colonel's mare five days before on this very ground. And it might be that knowing his carelessness had afforded the opportunity, the guard had not reported that I had pumped him for information, then attempted to escape with it. But these facts were almost certain to come out in the trial; and they would be much against me.

I was now taken across the fields to a place beside the big road where two or three Confederates and several Yankee soldiers had been assembled in a fence corner under guard. Regarding my situation as so critical, I determined not to let pass the least opportunity of escape. If by any chance the court-martial were deferred till night, I would make a run for the woods, there being quite a forest on the other side of the road. I was tortured with anxiety, for I considered the chances of my being freed by the court of the charge of spying were but small.

In the party of Confederates was one whom I saw looking at his silver watch, and I asked the hour. Then as time dragged so heavily for me, longing as I was for darkness to come on, I found myself asking the time so often that in apology for the trouble I caused, I told him the cause of my anxiety. He told me that his name was Ferneyhough, and that he belonged to the Fredericksburg Artillery.

The number of prisoners gradually increased, until now it was pretty large. About three o'clock they brought in a young Confederate, who took his seat apart from the rest, and appeared wrapped in thought. Soon after, we were placed in a column, two abreast, and marched along the big road, the newcomer and Ferneyhough being the couple just ahead of me. I saw them conversing together, and presently the stranger turned around and asked, "Is your name Benson?"

I said, "Yes."

"Well," he went on, "you needn't feel any apprehension about that case of yours. You will be regarded as a prisoner of war."

"How do you know?" I asked eagerly.

He changed places with my companion and replied, "I was brought up before them this morning, and after getting through with me, they asked if I knew a man named Benson. When I said no, they told me the circumstances of your capture and asked me what motive you could have in claiming to be a Union scout. I told them that I supposed you were some greenhorn, so scared at being hailed that you hardly knew what you were saying. I listened as they talked amongst themselves, and gathered that you would be considered a prisoner of war."

I thanked him, feeling that probably he had saved my life. I still feel so, for if he had not thus relieved my apprehension of being hanged as a spy, I might have made some reckless attempt to escape, which might well have been my last act on earth.

Marching along under escort of cavalry, my companion now told me about himself. He was Sergt. Ellison of Co. E 3rd Ala. Regt., a scout of Genl. Ewell's. After listening to some of his scouting exploits, I proposed to him that we attempt to escape together. He agreed, but said that there would be little opportunity before reaching Fredericksburg, because of all the woods having been cut down for fuel during the campaigns.

We met the Washington Heavy Artillery coming to the front, as my guard the night before had said. They were dressed in span new clothes, with guns and equipments of all kinds fresh as though just out of a bandbox, and even wore *white cotton gloves.* How our boys did jeer! Even our Union guards shelled them hot with ridicule, saying "Oh, yes, Johnny Reb'll have them white gloves and them fat knapsacks too!" (Blackwood afterwards told me what a fine time they had plundering the knapsacks of the Washington Heavy Artillery!) I saw also that day another body of troops fresh arrived in the field, which my guard had said would come—the Corcoran Legion.

Being marched thro' the camps, I was continually hailed on all sides with, "Hello, Johnny!", Johnny Reb being a national name they had given us. In being first thrown among them, I was surprised at the immense amount of cursing and blackguarding I heard going on everywhere. There was nothing like it in our camps. I heard oaths that I had never heard before in my life, and a man would, in mere sport, call another the vilest names—a style of language that would have brought a fight on his hands in Confederate camps, fifty times a day.

We were kept at Fredericksburg two or three days. Our prison was simply a small bare hill—knoll rather—at the foot of which was a spring, and was surrounded (spring and all) by a guard. There were a few federal prisoners among us. While here, it rained, and as I had no tent, no blanket, oilcloth, or overcoat, I lay on the bare, cold, wet ground, not even leaves under me, and slept in the rain. I shall never forget walking about in the little enclosure as tho' walking would give me blanket or shelter, or make the ground dry or stop the rain, and finally lying down just so, with my head on my arm, while the rain kept falling. But I slept.

Our next move was to Belle Plain. Under a guard of the same number, 25 of us were taken, the distance being 8 miles. We crossed the Rappahannock at F. on a pontoon bridge. The country was still all open, the trees on this side of the river having been cut down by the enemy for fuel in the winter of 1862-63, as on the other side had been done by our army.

At Belle Plain we were confined in a stable. Pretty soon a chaplain came in and began discussing slavery Abolitionism. Sergt. Ellison took up the argument, and being asked by the chaplain what was his rank, Ellison answered, "Captain."

Amongst our number was a N. C. soldier whom the boys, finding him a good subject, began to tease. They accused him of Union sentiments, of intention to take the oath of allegiance to the U. S. They said we intended to try him by court martial for this crime, and that we had already decided to find him guilty. I took no part in this, but Ellison did, advising the man to "break and run," saying that the "guard might miss," but that he would certainly be hung if he staid.

The sentry at the back of the stable heard scraps of this, especially "break and run" and "guard might miss," and inferred we were planning escape, and so reported to the guard, saying "That Captain is at the head of it," pointing to Ellison. The Sergt. of the guard, a tall, fine-looking fellow, in a black uniform (instead of blue) had been very kind to us, giving us his own rations when we could draw none. He now grew very angry, and gave the whole of us warning to drop that subject. In vain we told him the true circumstances; he believed his sentry. Shortly after, an officer came in, hand-cuffed Ellison, and took him away.

Next morning a new prisoner was brought in, who said the 8th Illinois Cavalry had him prisoner the night previous; and he had heard them talking about a Confed. Capt. having been taken handcuffed into the woods and hung. This cast a gloom over us all.

From the barn we were moved to the edge of a cleared hill, on top of which were some pieces of artillery, bearing on us. Our number was much increased, and we now drew rations for the first time in several days. We might have suffered severely for food, if our guards had not been good fellows and divided with us.

Belle Plain was a landing on the Potomac. Monday afternoon, May 23, 1864, about 500 prisoners were put on board a steamer and carried down to Point Lookout Prison, arriving about 4 p.m. There we were drawn up in ranks 16 deep, and answered to our names.

The prison was a rectangular enclosure of about ten acres, and was said to contain at that time about 10,000 prisoners. The soil, inside and outside, was white sea sand, and this with the white tents and whitewashed houses and fence, made in the sunshine a strong glare. Some men, I was told, lost their eyesight in consequence. They say that many, amongst both prisoners and guards, became afflicted with night blindness—that is, inability to see at all by night. I have seen soldiers on the march who could see as well as anybody in the daytime, being led by a comrade at night, unable to see a thing.

The fence around the prison was of upright planks, about ten feet high, and around the outside of it, about four feet from the top of the fence ran a raised platform for the sentries to walk on. In one end of this fence was a large gate through which went all communication with the outside world. This was kept shut. In the side of the prison fronting the Chesapeake were three smaller gates. Opposite them out in the Chesapeake about 25 feet from shore, stood three wooden boxes or privies, with walls about waist high. These were elevated on piles driven in the water, and were approached on wooden plankways leading from the beach.

The prisoners were allowed to go in and out of these three gates at pleasure all day, a line of sentries being placed at each end of the open space to prevent escape that way. At sundown, the gates were locked.

Inside the fence were rows of tents with streets between, and a number of buildings of rough pine whitewashed, used as kitchens, dining rooms, hospitals, etc. Outside the prison were a good many houses occupied by the guards, or used for storage, and a hundred other purposes. The camp was separated into Divisions and the Divisions subdivided into Companies. I was put in Co. H., 8th or maybe it was 9th Divn. In the tent where I was placed, were 15 others, and it may be well believed that 16 men, even in a Sibley tent, were badly crowded. It was a difficult matter to dispose ourselves to sleep.

Between Fredericksburg and Belle Plain I had made acquaintance with a few of my fellow prisoners, of whom I remember only Ellison, Ferneyhough, Savage (a Virginian in the Signal Corps) and Philip F. Russell (of Goochland County, Va.). I have told about Ellison's being taken away; the others I had hoped to continue in company with. But we were separated, and I now found myself with strangers—men whom I thought I could not affiliate with. I deposited my luggage—a blanket, half a blanket, and a Federal overcoat, which I had picked up, thrown away by Union soldiers. My tentmates told me that the half blanket and overcoat would be taken away from me on Sunday, inspection day. This was proper, for new prisoners would be coming in, some of them without anything, and it was no more than right that any surplus should be divided up.

It being yet some time before dark, I knocked around camp a little, wishing to survey the situation and get an idea of the prospects for escape.

Directly I was addressed by one whose face I remembered, though he had to tell me his name—Michael Duffy of Co. I, my regt. He brought up another member, who had been in prison with him since July 1863—ten months. The talk soon turned to escape and they told me that the night before a prisoner had dug a hole under the fence and escaped. The story seemed doubtful to me, as did other stories I heard about escapes made by tunneling out. As the whole formation of Point Lookout is loose sand, I doubt if any tunnel got more than a start.

Another story was of a boat patched together of cracker boxes and stray pieces of plank. This improbable structure was said to have been kept turned upside down in a tent, disguised as a bed, where it was found during a Sunday inspection before an opportunity offered for launching it. A more likely tale was of a swimming match in which two prisoners engaged. With sentries looking on, the contestants went further out at each trial until at last, when the gates were about to be closed, two heads were seen far out, of which only one returned, the other keeping out to sea until darkness came on, when presumably he swam to shore and made good his escape. Another tale was that on the beach while swimming and washing clothes, the men took one of the big wooden tubs (half of a barrel) to play with, and that when the gates were to be shut they came in, forgetting the tub. The sentries saw it floating far out to sea, upside down, but did not suspect that a prisoner went with it, his head under the inverted tub.

It was to the sea that I turned my attention as the best avenue of escape. But to fit myself I should have to perfect my swimming. I resolved to spend much of my time in the water, thinking that thus I might be prepared to undertake the feat in three or four weeks.

Duffy told me that the prison guard consisted of three groups (three regiments, it may have been), one white, two negro. A group went on duty early in the morning and remained 24 hours, the sentries being relieved every two hours, as on camp duty. We were given only two meals a day, breakfast at eight, dinner at two. As I had come in after two, I went to bed hungry.

Next day, Tuesday, May 24th, at the summons the ranks were formed and the company marched to the eating house, where we had a slight breakfast given us. After breakfast, I walked out on the beach, and seeing a number of men in the water, I went in too and swam out some distance into clearer water, that next the shore being somewhat muddy from the washing of the waves on the beach. I was glad to find myself able to swim with so much greater ease than in fresh water—a fact that everybody knows. I went in several times that day.

Sitting on one of the gangways that led up to the big boxes, I entered into conversation with a man who told me he was a Louisianian, a member of Hays's brigade, that he had been in prison here all the past winter, but had been exchanged just before the battles at Spottsylvania. Then in the battle of May 12th, he had been re-captured and brought back to the same prison. That was ugly luck. He told me a good many things about the prison, its rules, etc. He said that above the prison there were stakes in the water to which were fastened wires which communicated with the guards' quarters on shore, so that if a prisoner escaped and tried to pass up along the Bay he would touch the wires and sound an alarm.

During the day, I walked about the prison also, especially noticing a small drain which led under the fence at the N. E. Corner. I went into one of the buildings which was used as a chapel and schoolhouse, with Confederate preachers and teachers. I believe the ladies of Baltimore supplied the books; I remember "Caesar's Commentaries" among them. At 2 o'clock we had dinner, but it seemed to me very scanty. As a whole, I don't think Confederate prisoners suffered greatly for food, tho' we had none too much truly. Perhaps because I had been roughing it for so long I needed more food than quiet prisoners.

It was a curious sight to see, before many tent doors, different trades being plied, such as cobbling, perhaps some kind of small carpenter's work, and many that I don't remember now; but chief of all prisoners' work was ring making. Then there were little tables made of cracker boxes on which wares were displayed, while the seller sat behind on a stool. Many of the tables held only hard tack and tobacco cut into squares perhaps as large as a thumb nail and called "chews." Tobacco I found to be the medium of trade, the currency, and the "chew" was the unit thereof. But tobacco and hard tack had the same value—1 cracker equals one chew. A user of tobacco, feeling that he *must* have a chew, saves a cracker from his dinner (ill can he spare it!), walks up to an exchange table, deposits his cracker and takes up a chew, saying never a word, likely as not, the relative value is so well established.

The next day [May 25, 1864], just before sundown, I was sitting on the beach waiting for the Sergeant to come around to close the gates, when I was surprised to see the white guards around the prison being relieved by blacks. This was surprising because, as I had learned, the new guard always went on early in the morning. And the Sergeant did not come to close the gates as usual, though it was now almost sundown. By sunset nearly all the prisoners had gone to their quarters. It began to grow dusk. No Sergeant yet coming, my heart began to beat fast. It was still too light, but a little later perhaps—I went inside and hurried to my tent, hearing many as I passed talking about the gates' still being open. Unperceived by the new guards, the whole prison was in a low fever of excitement.

I put on my jacket and stockings and stuck my hat in my bosom inside my shirt. My shoes being thick-soled and heavy, I was afraid to take, as I expected to have a good deal of swimming. I went to the middle gate and stood in it, waiting for it to grow dark enough. Now and then someone passed me, going inside or out. A party of six passed out and went into the central box. Directly they came back, but just as they got to the lower end of the plankway, I saw the last man of the group squat down and dart under the plankway. I had seen another get under there a little while before. I now walked out, passing over the two men.

Inside the box, I turned around and saw four negro sentinels standing above the gate. Reaching down, I caught hold of one of the wooden pillars and slid down into the water. It was breast deep. Backing slowly, so that I might keep the box between me and the sentinels, I went into deeper and deeper water. When it came to my chin, I turned and began to wade up the Bay.

Being 30 or 40 yards from shore, and the darkness having increased greatly, I believed my head would not be seen above the water. I passed the upper end of the prison; I passed the guards' quarters, the water all the time up to my neck. Then I ventured closer in toward shore, where the water was breast deep, and later to where it was waist deep. Passing the guards' quarters, I saw a stake in the water. Curiosity prompted me to find out whether there were really any wires as the Louisianian had said. I waded up to it, felt all around, and found there were no wires. My stockings, getting filled with water, came partly off and draggled at my feet. I pulled them off and put them in my pocket, but one getting lost out, I threw the other away.

I was now a good way past the prison. The walking so far was easy for my bare feet, being fine smooth sand or clay. Suddenly a sharp pain struck. I was no longer on sand, but stumbling over raccoon oyster beds, the shells cutting my feet like knives. It could not have been worse walking over broken bottles. Stumbling on, I passed over the first oyster bed, glad to get my wounded feet again on the sand. But soon I struck another oyster bed. Setting my lips against the pain which must be endured, I hobbled on, reaching down to break off two or three with my hands. These I ate, biting the thin edges of the shells, so I could pull them apart and get at the meat.

I now drew nearer the shore where the water was only knee deep. But I found that my legs in passing one another splashed the surface, so I went out again until it reached my hips, which seemed to be the best depth. Behind me trailed a cloud of phosphorescent light, by which I could see as low as my knees. I could see little fishes too that came playing around me, each in his own circle of light.

I looked behind me. Far away lay the white walls of the prison. Out at sea were the lights of one or two passing ships. The moon had risen, but was veiled by heavy clouds. Despite my wounded feet, how happy I was! For I was free! I had escaped those four awful white walls and with care and labor I would soon be under the red flag again, again under the stars and bars!

I dared not come to land yet, for I heard a dog barking on the shore, and feared guards might be there. I waded on, the water growing deeper. Seeking shallower water, I turned more in towards the shore. As it continued to deepen, I turned square in. The water rose to my breast, then to my neck. A moment later, I was swimming. A few strong strokes, and I let down my feet. No bottom! I swam quite a distance before letting my feet down again. Still no bottom! Another good, strong swim, and down went my feet. Still deep water! A thought, a fearful one, shot through me. Maybe the tide was going out and I was being drifted out to sea. I swam hard for what seemed a long time. And when next I let down my feet, the tips of my toes touched sand. I stood so for a moment resting, then pulled into shallow water, relieved and thankful.

Pretty soon I had another fright. I was walking along steadily, not thinking of sharks, when all at once one came rushing at me from deep water, churning it into foam as he came. How I sprinted! Before you could say "Jack Robinson," I stood in water not half knee deep. And then didn't I feel cheap when the next shark came and the next, and I knew it was just the coming back of the tide, which had turned, and these were but the first waves. I made up my mind never to tell anybody about it.

Standing half leg deep in the Chesapeake, watching the retiring monsters of the deep, I figured that I had come nearly two miles from Point Lookout Prison. Breathing the fresh cool free air of Maryland, no bayonets, nor walls, nor obedience—only the fields and the woods, the sea and the sky, I suddenly felt proud. What I had planned and striven for nine days without ceasing, I had at last achieved. I was a free man once more, free to fight again under the stars and bars for the liberty of my country.

I now quit the sea. Along the beach ran a road, a fence on the other side. I crossed both and found myself in a grain field near a dwelling, which I avoided. Soon I came to a sheet of water, probably a quarter of a mile wide. I walked along its edge toward my left until it narrowed to only a marshy branch, and there crossed it. I came into another field where were a farmhouse and outbuildings. The field was strewn with broken oyster shells, which hurt my sore feet badly, and I hurried on to reach some woods which lay beyond. Before reaching them, I was stopped by a sheet of water about 200 or 300 yards wide, evidently an arm of the bay. Having walked up it some distance without finding any change in its breadth, I concluded to swim it. Just as I reached my foot forward to step into the water, I was brought back with a jerk by perceiving that I was about to step off a bank ten or twelve feet high. In the darkness, it had appeared to me that I was walking along the water's edge.

Farther up, I found it narrowed to about forty feet width. The water in mid channel was only breast deep. But how was I disappointed when I had crossed, to find before me yet another hundred yards of water. Apparently this was an island. On it were piles of split pine, in four foot lengths, evidently intended for fuel. I had heard in prison that details of prisoners were sometimes sent out under guard to cut wood for the prison, and I thought this was possibly prison work. Taking a stick of the 4 foot light pine under each arm, I went down into the water and made the passage. By the sparks in the water I knew it to be salt.

Landing, I climbed up a bank and found stretched before me another hundred yards of water. My landing place was but a point, whether of an island or the junction of two streams, I don't know. I have thought this might be St. Mary's river. Having swum this last stretch, I found myself amongst fallen trees, cut for fuel, and had much difficulty getting thro' them, for the broken twigs were constantly piercing my feet in the fresh cuts, so that every step was exceedingly painful.

Coming out of the woods into a field, I saw two horses; and at once I coveted one, longing for the relief that riding would give my wounded feet. I tried to catch one, but not succeeding, I went towards a house that I could see on a hill. Near one of the outhouses, I found an old pair of shoes, but they were so large and hard and stiff (having lain out in sun and rain till nearly rotten) that I could not bear them on my feet. I got into a small road and continued in it until it entered a larger public road, along which ran a telegraph line—the line from Washington to Point Lookout. Afraid to travel in it, I took to the by-roads and paths through the woods. Again I tried to capture a horse in a field, but after having his heels flourished around my head once or twice, I left him alone. Near daybreak, May 26, I was walking in a lane when I came upon two horses feeding. Approaching very cautiously, I caught one. He was facing the right way, and I sprang on his back. But no sooner was I mounted than he whisked around and carried me back at a gallop the way I had come. Having no bridle, I tugged at his mane and growled, "Whoa!" But he only sped the faster. Not daring to jump off because of the condition of my feet, I reached forward and seized his ear and gave it a wrench. He stopped. So did I. But the method of my dismounting I respectfully decline to state.

Painfully retracing my steps, I had passed a little beyond where I had caught my steed, when I saw before me at some distance the masts of a schooner. I knew this must be in the Potomac, which is here about eight miles wide. So I turned off to the right, thro' a gate opening to a field, and walked a little distance. Being very tired, I sat down in a fence corner. By me lay some old, torn clothing. I picked this up and tearing it into strips commenced binding up my bruised and bleeding feet. Whilst I was thus engaged, a little negro boy and girl came by, and seeing me, stopped and looked all the astonishment they must have felt.

Finding that I could not adjust the rags to my feet comfortably, I threw them away, disappointed that this effort to alleviate the pain of the hurts and bruises to my feet had also failed. The cuts had become filled with grit, and were so sore and tender that every step was attended with pain.

It was now near sunrise. I went to the cowpen and started talking with the negro children, trying to learn whether there were any Southern sympathisers about. The little girl, who was the elder, told me that at first nearly everybody was for the South, but now some of them had changed sides, and that her master had.

"How do you know?" I asked.

"I hears 'em talking," replied the child.

"Does anybody around here still hold out for the South?" I asked.

"Yessir, Mr. H - -."

"How do you know?"

"I hears him and my master arguing."

In response to questioning, she told me that Mr. H lived alone, that he was rich, and that his house was the third past something or other—I think it was past a mill. With high hopes of finding the succor I sorely needed, I followed her directions until I came to "the third house" past something or other. I think it was a mill. It was old, weatherbeaten, in the last stages of dilapidation. Certainly no rich man lived *there*. I passed on with a heavy heart. It may be that I had misunderstood the child's directions.

It now began to rain, which was in one way a benefit—it softened the road, making it easier to my feet. As for getting wet, I was already wet through, and had been since dark the night before. Though much fatigued, I continued to plod on, not stopping to rest long at a time. I traveled thro' the woods all I could, obliged to pick my way carefully, yet despite all my caution, I often stepped on things that hurt my feet. Once I got into such a maze of calico bushes, vines, and briars that I had to get on hands and knees and crawl.

About midday, the rain ceased and the sun came out. I stopped in a fence corner, and pulling off my jacket, spreading it out to dry, I lay down and slept some. I waked in the afternoon, feeling very hungry. Out in the field I saw two small boys. I put on my jacket and going to them, asked whether they had seen a stray horse, giving a description of one that I pretended to be looking for. They had not. I shifted the conversation gradually to the war, and was told by them that three men in the neighborhood were Southern sympathisers, one especially so. His house they pointed out in the distance. I left them, going off in another direction; but out of their sight, I turned and went to the house.

A lady, I suppose his wife, being in the room with the man, I hesitated to state my case, so I made inquiry again as to the horse, saying I had followed him farther than I had expected and was hungry, and asked if he would be so kind as to give me a little something to eat. He asked the lady to get something for me, and as soon as she stepped out of the room I told the man the truth. At once he said he was a Union man, and could give me nothing. I asked him not to inform on me. He replied that there was no one nearer than the Point to inform; that he was unwell and shouldn't go there. So I left, dinnerless and disheartened. I made a firm resolve not to betray myself to anyone again. This resolution I rigidly adhered to, though I think now that I made a mistake in not having bestowed confidence somewhere.

All that day and night I continued to walk, stopping to rest and sleep only at long intervals, and then for but a short time. In the night it rained. Walking along the road in the rain, I continually cast my eyes to one side coveting this or that spot to rest and sleep in. Once I passed a thick bushy tree with low overhanging boughs like a tent. It was dripping with rain and all underneath was saturated, but the bed of leaves looked so soft and the boughs came down in such a sheltering way that I said to myself, "How I would like to lie down and sleep here!" But with a resolution which I fear I do not possess now, I plodded on.

Sometime probably early in the night of May 26th, I came to a river which I took to be the Potomac. I now think it was the St. Mary's River and the town of St. Mary's. I looked along the banks for a small boat, but found none. Getting over into a garden, I pulled up some onions and stuck them in my pocket. I was very hungry, but had no appetite for raw onions. As day was beginning to break, I entered another town—Leonardtown, I think. Throughout the town I saw but one light, at a window. I passed a church on my right hand and directly was out of the town. Just outside I met a negro riding, who appeared to regard me with curiosity. No doubt, my personal appearance, barefoot, with Confederate uniform, was sufficiently striking. About a mile farther on, a man came riding from behind and passed me, followed by a negro riding—I think the same whom I had just before met. The negro turned and eyed me several times after passing. I thought I would better leave the road as it was getting so light.

As I was very tired I went off into a pine thicket on the right, and lay down in a little dry ditch or trench about 25 yards from the road. A log also intervening, I was pretty well hidden from the road. It was now about sunrise of Friday, May 27th. Now and then a cart would go by. Feeling quite hungry, I took out my onions and looked at them. A drink of milk the little negro children had given me and a couple of raw oysters had now been the only food I had had in 40 hours, and I had endured much fatigue during that time. Hungry as I was, it was with difficulty that I forced myself to eat two of the onions. The others I put back in my pocket.

Hearing a horse coming from toward the town, I looked up. There he rode, the man I had been all along on the lookout for—a Federal cavalryman! I lay low and watched. He passed and then following him at about 100 yards came four more, two abreast. As far behind them again rode four more—nine in all. Such an unusual order of riding meant business, and that business I interpreted as pursuit. I saw that I must leave that road and keep to the woods.

My traveling now became very painful. I was always stepping on stones and dead branches, which gave me great pain. And I grew exceedingly hungry. Passing a little marsh where I saw a number of frogs, I wished I had the means of making a fire that I might catch some and broil them.

I continued to walk until about noon, when I came to a little field, in which were a negro woman and her two children hoeing near their cabin. Deciding to venture, I went to her and asked about the stray horse. Of course she hadn't seen it. I then asked whether she would give me something to eat. Inviting me into her cabin, she fried a rasher or two of bacon and placed it before me, with some cold cornbread and cold coffee. Had my eyes been shut, I might possibly have been able to tell by the feel in my mouth, which was bread and which meat. But not by the taste, for my taste was completely gone, with my 48 hour fast. Altho' I ate heartily, I tasted nothing until near the end of the meal, I began to taste the bacon grease into which I was dipping my bread, having eaten all the meat.

While I ate, the woman told me that she was a Catholic, and that her husband, tho' temporarily absent, was afraid to go abroad much, his life having been threatened by a neighbor. Having finished, I thanked my black hostess and bade her goodbye, which I did very hastily, as I felt that the victuals would not rest upon my stomach. I restrained myself long enough to reach the woods (some 30 yards away) when I threw up the whole dinner, including the onions of that morning. A deathly sickness came over me. Feeling faint and weak, I managed to go a little way into the woods, where I lay down. But mosquitoes gathered on me so thick that I had to get up and move further away from the swamp. I lay down again, so completely exhausted that I did not move when I saw a big snake crawling toward me, passing right by my feet.

A faintness came over me and a sort of stupor. I never knew whether I was awake or asleep when I plainly saw three men walking toward me along a little path. I started up to run. There was the path, but no men—it was all imagination or a dream. After a little I began to feel much better. I think I had had fever, which now wearing off, left my head clear. But my limbs were weak and I walked slowly, feeling no hunger now, but knowing that I must eat to regain strength.

I had walked about a mile when I came to a small house where I saw a lady with a little child. To her I told my horse tale, concluding by saying I had got lost and was very hungry. She placed before me some cold broiled bacon, cornbread, milk, and butter. Fearing that the meat might make me sick again, I made my dinner off bread and butter and a glass of milk. While I ate, an old man came in and began asking questions, to all of which I found it necessary to give evasive replies. Finally he said, "I expect you are a deserter from Lee's army."

Though it had not occurred to me before, it now struck me that this might be an excellent role for me to play. So without saying so directly (for the words stuck in my throat) I gave such a reply as led him to think I was a deserter, afraid or ashamed to acknowledge it. At once he grew frightened, and declared that if the military authorities were to know I had been fed there, he and the lady would both be put in prison, citing a parallel instance that had happened in the neighborhood. I assured him that I didn't wish to get him into any trouble, and by continued representations of my alarm for his safety I so worked upon his fears as to induce him to accede eagerly to my proposal that neither of us should mention my having been there. He then urged me to go, directing me to the County road, and advising me earnestly to go straight to Leonardtown and take the oath of allegiance to the U.S. I seemed very willing and asked whether I should turn to the right or the left when I reached the road. He said left. But alas for the unreliability of human nature—when I found the road I turned to the right, and from that day to this I have never seen Leonardtown or the man that administers the oath.

I came to a branch—probably McIntosh Run or Brooks' Run—which I crossed, rolling up my breeches as I did when a boy. After a while I came to a field, a man in it plowing. It was now near sundown; and not wanting him to see me, and there being no way to flank him, I crept into a fence corner where concealed by bushes, I lay resting till he went home. I then crossed the field to the woods where I found a road, into which I jumped from a bank five or six feet high. This was a mistake from which my feet suffered.

As it was now dark and the road led through a great forest, I kept on it until sometime in the middle of the night, feeling very tired, I went a little way off it and lay down. I was about going to sleep when I heard horses' feet, and directly a rider went by at a swift gallop, traveling in the same direction as I was. It was so dark I could only see a dim form flit past; but I decided it would be safer to keep off the road. After a short sleep, I traveled on, keeping to the woods and fields.

I think it was Saturday, May 28, 1864 that my road led through an immense forest, probably the country north west of Hollywood. For miles I saw no fields or habitation. In the forenoon, I grew very hungry. I tried to eat a raw mushroom but could not, so I ate a few green huckleberries. None of the wild fruits were ripe. Finally I came into what appeared to be a plantation road. About noon, I stopped at a house and asked for something to eat. The lady gave me some bread and bacon. She also gave me some matches that I asked for (six) to light my pipe. These I put away to kindle a fire. Sometime during the night of the 28th, I entered a chestnut wood, and it may well be conceived that I suffered much by stepping on the fallen burrs with my wounded feet. There I lay down to sleep, kindling a little fire of dry limbs to keep me warm. Every now and then I would wake from the cold, and get up and replenish the fire.

I got up at sunrise (Sunday, May 29th) and was sitting down leaning against a tree when I saw walking thro' the woods, a man followed by a little girl. The man passed close by, but did not see me. Nor did the little girl until she got quite close. Then she stopped still and gazed at me. I kept perfectly still, hoping she would pass on, but she continued staring. And so she staid till the man was out of sight. Then she began quietly to get behind a tree. The man, missing her, now began to call her. She made no answer. Knowing now that the man would return for her, I got up and walked quickly away. The little girl must have been considerably frightened, no doubt associating me with all the giants, ogres, Bluebeards and what-nots that she'd ever heard about. I had wanted very much to try to comfort her but had dared not, fearing any move I should make would increase her fright.

In a little while I came to a house and ventured to go up and ask for something to eat. A man was sitting in the yard. He called to his little daughter to bring a chair for me, and while his wife prepared some breakfast, he questioned me. I told him that I was a deserter from Lee's army (it didn't choke much now), and that I was on my way to Washington to take the oath. He asked my reason for deserting, and now my solid loyalty to the cause fought against my denying my country even in seeming. I replied, "I quarreled with my Captain, and finally struck him. Being arrested, court-martialed, and sentenced to imprisonment, I managed to escape and deserted." This story I repeated ever after when questioned, it reflecting no blame on the Confederacy.

The lady brought me some warm cornbread, broiled

fish, and plenty of milk and butter, and wrapped some food in a clean cloth and gave it to me to take with me. She also brought out a pair of socks, saying they had no shoes to spare, but maybe I could get shoes from some-one else. Moved by their kindness, I was sorely tempted to tell my true history, but I kept firm. I think now that I ought to have told.

I thanked the couple heartily for their kindness and departed, but the gentleman said he would go with me to the road he advised me to take. We passed a house where an elderly gentleman was sitting on the porch, and as he appeared curious, my guide walked towards him and said something, obviously about me. I think he said that I claimed to be a deserter, but that he thought I was an escaped prisoner. Anyhow, the old gentleman called to me, "Better mind how you travel. I saw two cavalrymen pass here this morning."

Coming in sight of the road I was to take, my guide wished me good luck and left. At the fork of the road some negroes watched me attentively, and as I walked away one began to sing "Dixie." Once before in a field someone had started singing "The Bonnie Blue Flag" as I passed. A little past the fork, I met a carriage in which were two men. As I passed, I asked, "Is this the road to Washington?"

They answered, "Yes."

They had passed me about 30 yards, I suppose, when one of them put his head out and called back to me, "There are soldiers stationed up on the hill there," and drove on.

Immediately I left the road and took to the fields, more than half wishing the carriage had stopped and given me a chance to confide in the men. The country was quite hilly, and in places the fields were covered with stones and gravel. It was such torture to my feet that coming to a house, I ventured to ask for a pair of shoes. I was met by a young man who stammered badly. Of an exceedingly obliging disposition, he began to exhert himself at once to find me a pair. After a little he brought shoes which, though worn, were yet quite serviceable. Apologizing for their condition, he said he had neglected to clean them after his last fishing trip, that he was sorry he hadn't a better pair etc. etc. But I was only too glad to get these and expressed my gratitude accordingly. He gave me some directions as to traveling and I left.

Having now shoes and stockings, I stopped at the first stream I came to, and washed my feet well and long, picking the sand out from the cuts with a needle, and greasing them with some of the fat bacon the lady gave me this morning. I also washed my shoes of the mud, and greased them to make them soft. Then I put them on and they fit me nicely. Oh how proud I felt, and how comfortable! Then I washed my face and combed my hair, cocked my hat to one side, and shuffled on, no longer barefoot, though the shoes hurt my sore feet some, of course.

Traveling in the road, I met a carriage, in which were some ladies—returning from church, I suppose. As I passed they looked at me with considerable attention, which seemed to deepen into marked interest. Then as I lifted my hat with a graceful bow, they—they bowed in return! To me, a poor ragged dirty devil whose only claim to recognition from them was the grey jacket I wore. Why did I not stop and say, "Ladies, I am in trouble. I belong to Lee and am trying to get back to him. Can you not help me?"

I had said I would not ask for help. And I suppose it is true that I am obstinate. I think this happened near a little place called Charlotte Hall, and I believe it was after dark that I passed through Beantown. It was still early in the evening when I was overtaken by two little negro boys who volunteered the information that they were looking for—a horse! I was immediately suspicious. My previously practiced deception rose in judgment before me. But I kept on with the boys, until coming to a gate across the road, they found their horse and left me.

My way now lay along the Telegraph Road, which I followed by the posts. After traveling a long time, I missed the post and concluded I had taken a wrong turn somewhere. I decided to go off in the woods and sleep some. When I woke, it was after sunrise, Sunday May 30/64. I now saw why I had missed the posts. They ran thro' the field, making a short cut at a bend in the road. I ate a light breakfast out of my cloth, still keeping back a little. Then I traveled on, keeping in sight of the telegraph poles.

Learning now, by asking, that I was within 20 miles of Washington, I determined to go to the river and see how things looked. I therefore turned to the left, down a creek which must have been the Piscataway, crossed on a log to its right bank, and kept down it. Soon it began to widen rapidly, from which I judged that I was close to the river. Directly, from the top of a low hill, I saw it, with schooners and other small vessels on it, both in motion and at anchor. I kept up the river, going over many hills, high and steep.

About 3 P.M. I climbed a tall chestnut tree on top of one of the highest hills, to take a survey. When I reached the top, I had a fair view of the Potomac, and could see vessels of many kinds going up and down. Upriver on the opposite side I saw a city, which I knew must be Alexandria. To the right of it, and seeming to rise out of the river was a monument— the unfinished Washington monument. Farther to the right, looming above the tree tops, was a great white dome—the dome of the Capitol. Resting comfortably on a limb, I caught myself near dozing.

Before sunset I came down from the tree and ate the remainder of my provisions. Making my way up the river, I heard drums beating, and on the river bank I saw a fort, apparently built of stone, and there a band began to play. Afraid of being seen, I got into a gully lined with trees and bushes, and protected thus I walked a good distance, until I came to a place where a marsh full of weeds and water-lillies barred my way upriver. I thought it would be too far to go around this marsh, so I waded across, the width being about 60 yards, and the mud in some places about knee deep. I had to cross three or four of these marshes one after another. Then I found myself on a neck of land between the Potomac and the marshy creek I had just crossed—It must have been Swan Creek—which emptied into it. At its mouth, the creek was probably a quarter of a mile wide, and across it, now below me was the fort—Fort Washington, about fifteen miles below Washington city.

Exhausted, I had lain down to rest, when a man came up to drive away two horses that were feeding near. He saw me and looked surprised, continuing to regard me attentively without speaking. I saw that I had better do or say something as an excuse for being there, so I asked if he could tell me how to get over to the fort.

"You can't get over there now," he replied. "What do you want to get over there for?"

"To get work."

"Why don't you get work from somebody over here?" he demanded, and went on to tell me that he was overseer at a nearby plantation where there was plenty of work, asking whether I could do gardening.

When I replied that I could, he offered me a job at eighteen dollars a month. I said I thought I could do better than that, whereupon he replied scoffingly that other people were offering no more than $10. Replying that I should *try* to get more at some houses I had passed, I started off towards Washington. Once out of his sight, I turned off towards the river, and lay down within sight of it, debating with myself whether I should attempt passage here, or go up perhaps as far as Leesburg, where the Potomac was narrower and shallower and where I had a friend, Judge Gray, who would help me. Here the river was wide—a mile or more, I suppose, for the trees looked very small on the other side. But to go to Leesburg, I would have to pass around Washington, a long circuit in Maryland, passing through dangerous country between Washington and Baltimore, and I was tired and my feet were sore.

The fact that swimming the Potomac was the "short cut" to Virginia, where I would be in my own country, decided me, and I did not wait long after coming to my decision. If I had felt strong, I should probably have entered the water and made a bold, unaided swim for the opposite shore, but worn out as I was, prudence dictated that I would better take such help as I could get. It was now quite dark. I went to a fence nearby and from a short panel I took two rails some 5 or 6 feet long. Placing them on the ground, parallel to one another and about 18 inches apart, I tied them in this position at both ends. The cord I tied them with I had picked up on the side of the road a day or two before. I had passed it some little distance when I thought, "Benson, that string may do you some good service," and back for it I went.

Taking from my pocket the string with which the lady had tied the package of food, I tied my five remaining matches strongly in the middle of it. Placing the matches on the crown of my head, I tied the end of the cord under my chin. This way, if any inch of me landed dry on the other side, the matches would, and I would need a fire to dry and warm myself. I folded up my hat and put it in my bosom and buttoned my jacket close. I did not remove any of my clothes—not even my shoes. They were light, and I could not bear to part from them. Launching my two rails quietly, I got between them, one under each arm, and waded off from shore. In a few yards, I was swimming.

The rails were not large enough to hold me above water when I kept still, but were a great help. Having free use of my hands, I could make fair progress. Though I aimed for a point of woods on the opposite shore, I expected that the current would drift me below it. But the water seemed to be nearly still; perhaps the tide was coming in and so counteracted the current. My rails *would* slip forward, however, and after shifting them back several times, I let them alone, the cord across the hinder end pressing against my back, the two foremost ends coming nearly together in front.

I had not got far when the cord across my back suddenly snapped, the rails slipped from me and began to float off. A few strokes enabled me to regain them, but now, the cord being broken, I was obliged to hold onto the rails with my hands, propelling myself only with my feet. Directly I saw a schooner with all sails set coming up the river, headed right towards me. Whether it would pass in front or behind or over me, I could not tell. As I watched anxiously, I saw it would pass behind me, very close.

Near the middle of the river, a rowboat came along, going up stream, two men in it rowing. As it drew close, the men saw me and held up their oars, the boat gliding on. They began talking in a low tone, and I recognized their voices as negroes'. With my head as low as possible in the water, the ends of the two rails sticking out in front, I knew the men were regarding me closely. Keeping perfectly still, I had the great satisfaction as they passed of hearing the one word, "Log," which seemed to me at that moment the sweetest word in the English language.

Soon after this adventure, cramp seized my left leg. Alarmed, I kicked hard, and the cramp left me. Not long after, I saw a steamboat coming up the river, lit from stern to stem with lights, white and red. A beautiful sight, as I knew, even when it seemed about to pass over me. But I had the satisfaction of seeing it, too, pass close behind me, while I rode up and down, up and down on the waves in its wake. This was my last danger. I soon drew near the point of woods that I had been swimming for. After one or two trials, letting down my feet, I was able to touch bottom, and my long swim was over. I was on Virginia soil—my own country! This was near Mt. Vernon.

I climbed up a steep bank and went some distance into the woods to make a fire. Gathering some sticks, I tried to strike a match, but it was wet. But the second match lit, and I soon had a low, hot fire, and lay down before it, taking off some of my clothes and spreading them and my testament before it to dry. Then I slept.

When dawn came, I took up the line of march, though my clothes had not dried out much during the night. Passing a house, I took to a plantation road, but quitted it for some pine woods, to dodge a man I saw with a gun. At length I brought up in a field against a lagoon about 30 yards wide. Hunting a place to cross, I came to a boat with a paddle in it, but close by was a man plowing. He had his back to me, or he might have seen me take his boat. I was soon on the other side, where I had to resort to Jacksonian tactics, winding amongst hollows and sneaking behind bushes in an almost open field, to avoid being seen by some half dozen men plowing.

Coming out upon a high road, I passed a stately residence where I saw an elderly gentlewoman talking to a man who seemed to be the overseer, apparently giving instructions about the grounds, which were ornamented with flowers and shade trees. I passed unobserved, but had not got far when I heard horse's hoofs behind me. I jumped over the fence into some woods and lay down. The man passed—the same whom I had just seen. I staid there some time debating whether I ought not go back and tell my story to the lady. Finally deciding against it, I traveled on, and after a while encountered a lady with two children. I asked the way to Alexandria (though actually wishing to go in the opposite direction). She told me but advised me to be careful, as the citizens throughout that neighborhood arrested all strangers.

So I went into the woods and lay down in a spot of sunshine, pulling off my coat to dry. Here the ticks seemed determined to eat me up or carry me off. Both here and in Maryland they swarmed. I remained here till late in the afternoon, watching passengers and vehicles on the road, myself hidden. By their number, I thought I must be near a village. I intended keeping close till night, but chafed so at the delay that I decided to risk a little daylight, keeping to the woods and fields.

Walking thro' the woods, I came to the brow of a hill, below which lay a narrow valley, a stream thro' it. Where the stream crossed the road was a wooden and brick mill and several other houses. Deciding to circle around and cross the valley below this settlement instead of above, I was walking along a little by-road in the woods, when two boys came in sight, one about 18, the other about 12. Immediately, the eldest called out, "Halt!" Knowing that it would not do to run or in any way appear to shun them, I walked towards them, apparently unconcerned.

"Where are you going?" the elder demanded.

I told him that I was looking for work, and after a little talk, he said that the miller wanted to hire someone, and that he would show me the way. In vain I urged him not to trouble himself, that I could follow his directions; he *would* go. Realizing that in my present condition, I could not outdo the two boys, either in a fight or a footrace, I saw no resource but to go with them, hoping the miller would be some old codger whom I could manage to fool.

Far from an "old codger," the miller turned out to be a big strapping fellow of about 35, with a pistol buckled round his waist. In reply to his questioning, I told him I was from Alexandria, a carpenter by trade. Quickly informing me that my hands showed no signs of carpenter's work, he asked, "Who is Provost Marshal, in Alexandria?" When I had to confess that I didn't know, he said, "I thought so. Now tell who you are."

"I am a deserter from Lee's army," I said.

Not accepting this either, he put me through some sharp questioning as to how I had got here, where I had got so wet, the appearance of the Occoquan river, which I claimed to have swum, finally demanding, "Are you one of Kincheloe's men?"

"I don't even know who Kincheloe is," I answered—this time speaking the truth.

I was informed that Kincheloe was a rebel guerrilla, operating on the lower Potomac as Mosby operated on the upper. I learned that the miller was a New Jersey man named Troth, who had raised a company of home guards (he claimed 300 in number) to resist the depredations of guerrillas. By his band he was called Captain Troth.

With a sinking heart, I realized that I had toiled and

suffered so for the past 6 days, through the length of the partly hostile state of Maryland to reach the safety of my own country, and there I had fallen into the wrong hands! I determined that I would spare no effort or risk to again escape and reach the guerrilla band of which I was accused of being a member, even though I had never heard of Kincheloe.

Capt. Troth then asked me if I would have some supper. Not having eaten a mouthful all day, I thanked him and went with him to his house. The supper was very light, only some cold light bread, a little chipped dried beef, and a cup of tea. The Capt. then put me in the charge of the young man who had captured me (named Williamson). My guard, pistol in hand, took me to the blacksmith shop, where was a little crowd gathered. The blacksmith, a pleasant man, began asking me questions. After listening to me talk, and especially after having me repeat the word "do" several times over, he said I looked like a Southerner and talked like one. He then asked if I would care for a glass of milk. I accepted his offer with thanks, and he brought me a bowlful, with some bread, which I ate. And now, although I had had as much as was good for me, my appetite still remained keen. So when my guard was called to supper and asked me to share it with him, I accepted his invitation, and we dined heartily on catfish stew.

My guard, Williamson, told me that this place was called Accotink. We had just finished supper, and it was growing dark when there came running by, white and black, helter-skelter, armed with all sorts of firearms, quite a number of men. In a minute, Capt. Troth rushed in demanding, "Where's that man?"

"Here I am, sir."

"Look here, didn't you tell me there was nobody with you?"

"Yes, sir, that's just what I told you."

"Well, it better prove so!" and off he ran, after the rest.

The tone in which he said the last words was very threatening, and I felt anxious until the party returned. Then it turned out that in the dash a man had been seen whom nobody knew. An alarm was given and pursuit made, when he proved to be one of their own men. The Capt. then had me removed to the mill and placed in an upper room in which were several Enfield rifles and sabres. Several Yankee overcoats were spread on the floor for me to lie on and I was told to make myself comfortable. As the Capt. went out he said, "I advise you not to jump out of the window." When he had gone, I went to the window, looked out and determined to take his advice. The ground, sixty feet below, was a bed of rocks.

My young captor and a negro remained in the room as a guard. They stuck a candle in a bottle, pulled out a greasy pack of cards, and prepared to pass the night. I went to sleep.

Sometime in the night I was awakened by the Capt. standing over me shouting, "Sit up. Let's have a look at you!" Turning to several men standing by, he asked, "Do you know him?"

As I sat up, they all shook their heads, saying, "No, it's not him."

"Well, gentlemen, if you're satisfied, I'll go to sleep again," I said, lying down.

About 1 o'clock I was wakened again and taken to the road, where I was turned over to a body of the 8th Illinois Cavalry. I was mounted on a horse, the second horse in a file of 4, my guard being just on my left hand, and two riderless horses on my right. There was a long column of these, and I supposed that a detachment had ridden somewhere to watch or fight on foot, the horses being sent back, for each man had four horses to take care of, the halters of the riderless being fastened each to the bit of the horse on its left. So I held no bridle, my horse being haltered to my guard's horse.

"Keep a good watch on him; he's pretty sharp," said Capt. Troth as we started off. And so my guard did, keeping his pistol in hand the entire way. I continued on the watch for a chance to escape, but he never relaxed his vigilance. Besides, I would have had to escape not only him, but the whole line of horsemen.

At daybreak, June 1, 1864, we reached Alexandria, and I was conducted to the office of the same Provost Marshal ignorance of whose name had so handicapped me when interviewed by Capt. Troth. When questioned, I told him my true name and regiment, thinking there was little fear here that they might point to my escape from Point Lookout. I stuck to my story of being a deserter from Lee's army, though he made every effort to break it down, trying to prove that I was one of Kincheloe's guerrillas. Finally he went to his desk and proceeded to write on a slip of paper. Standing in front of the desk, I had to read his writing upside down, and his wasn't such a good hand either. It said:

"Provost Marshal's Office, Alexandria, Va.

June 1, 1864.

Dear Capt. Brown: You will confine Berry Benson, a guerrilla, in the Lower Jail until further orders. W. F. Smith, P.M. etc."

The names are fictitious. I have forgotten the true ones. No evidence had been produced at any time to substantiate the description of me as a guerrilla. Having been handed this order for my imprisonment, my guard conducted me to the regular City Jail, a large gloomy looking brick building with ironwork at all the windows.

In the passage which we entered was a sentry, and three or four boxes of hardtack, one of which was open. While waiting, I pocketed some of the hardtack, with the guard's permission. I was taken thro' a door, which was closed on me and locked. I found myself in a narrow passage, with a brick floor. It was lighted by one grated window, and occupied by about 20 prisoners, Confederates and Yankees, some of them playing cards. Soon breakfast was brought to the door, one man bearing a large tin vessel of coffee, another a box of hard tack, and a third a tin pan full of boiled salt pork cut into convenient pieces. As the roll was called, each man who had a cup came forward and had it filled with coffee. No matter how big or little, it was filled, but the cupless had to do without. But I borrowed a cup from a man who had finished, and got some too. After the coffee, the pork was distributed—a piece to each. Then we were called up to get our hardtack, each man helping himself, some taking two or three pieces, some a handful. I held out my hat—a high crowned cavalry hat that I had picked up on the field on the eighth of May. The man poured crackers into it till they ran on the floor. Not knowing when I was going to get more, I determined not to waste them. So I set the hat carefully on a window sill.

As soon as everybody had finished breakfast, someone proposed that we sweep up. As though in indignant answer to such a suggestion, a cracker went sailing through the room. This was a signal for a general battle. Crackers, chunks of fat pork, shoes flew in all directions, while brooms were flourished as battle flags, or brought down as war clubs, nearly every man being engaged. In the midst of the fray a fellow made a dash upon my hat as it sat on the window sill, and the crackers rained. When he had emptied the hat, he thanked me for the loan of it, and replaced it in the window, and was presently engaged with his companions in sweeping the scattered bread and pork into a corner.

The fight being all in fun, there followed a friendly game or two of seven up. I now found why the men were so desirous of getting rid of the hardtack. As soon as it was all gone, the diet would be changed to baker's bread, which they liked better. I thought with a sad heart of all this destruction and waste of food by men, many of whom were under arrest for desertion, theft, and other crimes, when so many good men in our dear little faithful army would have been glad to take it up from the corner into which it had been swept.

Turning my attention at once to the chances of escape, I first explored my present quarters. The prison was a rectangular building with a passage running around three sides of it, the entrance being at one end of this passage; and the cells were inside, their doors opening into the passage. There being too many prisoners for the cells, the passage was occupied also, those who had blankets spreading them on the brick floor.

After breakfast we were turned out in the yard for an hour for exercise, the yard being small with a high brick wall around it. After dinner, another hour's recess was given. All the prisoners being given this freedom at the same time, I saw many who were kept in other rooms, some of whom were citizens, mostly from Virginia. Among these one especially attracted my attention. He was an old man, past eighty, and he always came outside with a chair and a newspaper or his Bible. His name was Calvert, and I learned that he had been offered his freedom if he would take the oath of loyalty to the U.S. He had replied that he would die first. I felt my heart warm toward this old man for his loyalty and heroism. Amongst the prisoners was a youth, not yet of age, dressed in Confederate uniform. He told anyone asking him that he had belonged to both armies, even telling it upon court martial, not having sense enough to know it was a serious matter. But his weak-mindedness was a safeguard. Soon he was turned out and told to go wherever he pleased.

A day or two after my arrival, some new prisoners were brought in, amongst whom were several of Mosby's men. I was particularly struck with the appearance of one of them, a tall fine looking man, about 24 years old. Observing that he and Mr. Calvert were acquainted, I asked Mr. Calvert some questions about him. Then I told Mr. Calvert my whole story, saying I wanted to know his friend, hoping that we might together devise some means of escape. The old gentleman was delighted to know that I was not really a deserter, and said I might trust Ben Crowley to any extent. So I came to know and like Crowley. But very soon I was moved into an upper room thus separated from him. I was now in detestable company, with gambling, cursing, and vile language going on all day and late into the night. This was the City Jail, ordinary criminals being mixed with prisoners of war.

On the morning of June 5, 1864, Crowley, three others, and I were put on a steamer and carried up the river to Washington. In the Provost Marshal's office there, I had the satisfaction of learning that there were no charges against me, and that I would be regarded simply as a prisoner-of-war. At once I dropped the "deserter" story, which was very disagreeable to tell. We were carried into the Old Capitol Prison.

It was June 5, 1864 when I first saw the inside of the Old Capitol—a prison that grew famous during the war. It was a large brick building with a great many rooms, all numbered. I was first put in a large room on the west side in the second story. It had a big arched window, which looked straight across to the Capitol, where on top of the dome stood the figure of Liberty, facing us.

I was soon acquainted with a number of my roommates, amongst whom was Wm. L. Royall, a Virginian, handsome and scholarly, belonging to the best type of Southern people. He was a member of Wickham's Brigade of Cavalry. Being of the same age and similar tastes, we were soon friends, and telling one another of our adventures. The talk inevitably turning to escape, Royall told me of two unsuccessful attempts he had made to escape from the Old Capitol. First, with a number of others in a room overlooking a side street, he had tried to get out by means of blankets tied together and let down from a window, but they were discovered by a sentry. Then, pretending to be sick, he was admitted to the hospital, where he managed to secure a large strong pair of scissors from the hospital supplies. He had just loosened the first brick from a wall, when in came a nurse. Though a Confederate prisoner himself, the nurse had treacherously reported him. He was then placed in solitary confinement in a cell narrow and dark, with a brick floor. After being kept here for some time, he was visited by an official who promised release from the dungeon upon his taking oath that he would not again attempt to escape. Though at first refusing, Royall finally could stand it no longer and gave the oath. He now seriously considered going to the officials and re-tracting this oath. He believed that if he could secrete a knife in his boot leg before being returned to his dungeon, he could dig his way through a wall to the kitchen, and thence escape.

Darkness coming on, and there being no lights, everybody prepared to go to sleep. Now I took it as a great sign of friendship that Royall insisted upon giving up his bunk to me, there not being enough bunks to go around. Ignoring my refusal, he vacated it, spreading his blanket on the floor. As I lay in the bunk, I heard a voice from the floor inquire, "How is it up there, Johnson?"

A voice from above replied, "It's gettin too hot for me; this bunk is chock full."

Another voice put in, "You're mighty right; I'm goin to try the floor," and a dark figure could be distinguished descending from a bunk, with blanket trailing over sundry faces as he picked his way among the men, and thereby evoking a good many dictionary words.

At first I couldn't conceive what the men were talking about, but I soon found out. Crawling over me, crawling over bunks and blankets, over walls and floors and men was such an army of bedbugs as I never saw in my life, before or since, all put together. There were hundreds; there were thousands; the bunks swarmed. The floor was somewhat better but not much. They were the standing joke of the prison, and I don't doubt that every man who ever was there will remember to his last day the bedbugs of the Old Capitol. Having no blanket, I lay down on the floor, and with my head on my arm, I somehow slept.

Next morning at the summons to breakfast, the guards opened the door, and we went pouring out, forming two ranks in the yard. When the dining room door opened, the head of the column marched in. But those in the rear, partly from being hungry, but more in a spirit of mischief, pressed the column forward, so that ranks were broken by the pressure. I was still some two yards from the door, mashed in on all sides, unable to move an arm, when I felt myself lifted off my feet by the pressure, and literally carried thro' the doorway, my feet not touching the ground. Meals had to be eaten in three relays, and the lucky ones getting in the first group had more time to spend walking around the yard before we were all returned inside. My surprise may be imagined when I here encountered Ellison, whom I had last seen taken handcuffed from the barn at Belle Plain. The report that he had been taken handcuffed into the woods and hanged may have been a rumor founded simply on his having been seen taken along handcuffed, or it may have been circulated deliberately by our guards in an effort to discourage attempts at escape.

Ellison was here in a room especially appropriated to officers, and with him was Capt. Wm B. Young, an old schoolmate of mine at Griffin's school. As officers were treated more liberally than privates in the way of rations, I was not too proud to accept from Ellison and Young the surplus food which they would save and bring out to me from time to time. But soon they were taken away, I believe to Ft. Delaware.

In my room were some of Kincheloe's men, and from them I learned much in regard to the border in Virginia that would have been very useful to me a week before. A good many of Mosby's men were prisoners here also. Besides Crowley, I came to know Woodhouse and Sam Underwood. These men of Mosby's were of better material than the average of soldiers, and had they been in the main army many of them would have been chosen as officers. There was a young cavalryman here, who had lost his arm in some battle, but come back into the service and had now been captured. He said he got along in camp or on the march as well as anybody, but that in a charge he had to take the reins in his teeth in order to handle pistol or sabre. I used to like to sit and hear Mosby's men talking about their raids. They said "Old Moss" (as they called their commander) sometimes got credit for deeds he had no hand in, they being planned and executed by some of the wild spirits among his men, who wouldn't keep quiet.

Most of the stories of escapes told here were of Mosby's men. One was that carpenters having been admitted to do some necessary work, a prisoner, as they were going home, picked up one or two tools and walked boldly out at the open gate, not even questioned by the sentry. Another one was that one of Mosby's men once walked unconcernedly past all the guards in the house, and at the front door, without even a glance at the guard there, walked carelessly out, and was not once halted, the very impudence of the thing making it successful. I was constantly studying my surroundings, searching for some avenue of escape as yet untried and therefore not so strictly guarded against. Finally I bethought myself of the hospital, above the dining room. So one day I played sick and went up. As I waited at the head of the stairs, I tried to imprint the surroundings on my memory. When the Doctor called me up, I gave such alarming symptoms that he administered a horrible compound of castor oil and something else, which I was obliged to take in his presence. Tit for tat! I went downstairs and washed out my mouth with soap and water, and didn't know whether my information had come cheap or not.

As days passed on and I saw no opportunity of escape, I began to chafe with impatience and anxiety. I harbored all kinds of schemes, dreaming of escape, and of my beautiful red banner. But as one scheme after another had to be abandoned as not feasible, escape seemed further and further away, and I began to fall into the worn, monotonous rut of every-day prison life. To get up in the morning, eat breakfast, then dinner, then after pacing the room an hour or two, lie down to sleep. All this time my health kept good and my appetite keen. Indeed, there was no time that I could not have eaten double the quantity given me. I forget just what the diet was at this prison, except that bean soup, of which I was quite fond, was a principal dish. Salt pork I suppose we got, maybe sometimes beef in the place of it, and bakers-bread or hard tack. Coffee we had until the 4th of July; then it was stopped. I suppose it was intended we should celebrate the day somehow. It was an interesting sight to see the men go in to meals. A double line, marching in at the door, divides, one half to one side of the table, the other to the other, taking seats on the benches and closing up so as to bring a plate opposite each man, the plates having been already provided with food, upon which all fall to. Sometimes by not closing up properly an effort is made to get a plate in between two, with nobody to take it, but the waiters at the table generally catch the trick and compel a closing up, to fill the place, or, if the men have already commenced eating, then the plate is removed. (All the plates, cups, and spoons, are tin and iron.) When the trick is successful, as it sometimes is, then the two between whom the extra plate falls, slyly divide its contents. All the men were not hearty eaters however, or sometimes there were those at the table who were not feeling well, so it often happened that these left half their food in their plates, which was thereupon, without shame or ceremony, appropriated by some neighbor whose appetite was better. Indeed, the scantiness of our fare was so generally admitted, and was the cause of such a prevalent wish for an increase in it, that when one at the table did not finish his plate, he would unhesitatingly pass it to some particular friend, who he knew would thank him for it, and that without blushing.

About this time I became acquainted with William F. Baxter of the 35th Va. Cavalry, the son of Judge S. S. Baxter of Richmond. We soon became fast friends, agreeing to work together upon any scheme of escape which seemed to us feasible. Baxter knew the upper Potomac very well; he had friends about Leesburg and elsewhere, and he knew some private fords, in all probability unguarded. We took into our confidence a fellow prisoner named Atkinson, and soon afterwards another, Robert Adams. Being removed to a room on the first floor, with only the cellar below, the thoughts of all naturally turned at once to cutting a hole in the floor, getting into the cellar, and making our way from there.

Under the bunk occupied by Baxter and myself, which sat some 12 or 14 inches from the floor, I began work. So as to drown the noise of the work as much as possible, lest there be some oath-taker in the room who would report us, the others undertook to set up a counter-noise, and did so pretty effectually. Singing, getting up lengthy debates and arguments, drumming on the floor etc., they were unwittingly assisted by some of the men who were ready to be merry and boisterous on all occasions. Once just as the whole crew happened to fall silent at the same moment, we got a scare, for my knife at that same moment slipped, making a rasping noise on the floor. But Atkinson covered up cleverly by saying, "The rats are making a heap of fuss tonight." But we had hardly got a good start on this project when we were moved to a room upstairs.

Early in July, there came a great excitement amongst us. From papers smuggled in we got the news that a large Confederate force had crossed the Potomac. Next day it was said to be only a small marauding party. But the next day the papers had it a bigger force than ever, a large Confederate army marching on the Capitol. The accounts kept see-sawing so that we didn't know what to believe. Finally it became clear that it was no mere raiding party, but a Confederate army under General Early, and that he was marching upon Washington. Papers were now kept strictly from us, our guards were strengthened, and we were watched closely. Soon prisoners began to come in, captured from Early. The authorities tried to keep them apart, to prevent their communicating with us. But still we managed to get the news from them. Finally Early stood in line-of-battle before the outer works of the city. We could hear his guns! From their room on the north side, Mosby's men could see his shells burst.

Our excitement was now at fever heat. We talked low, in groups. We made plans and combinations. We were 600 men, and we made plans to seize our guards, arm ourselves with their guns, and double quick to the works, attacking the enemy in the rear. Standing at the window, we saw the motliest crowd go by, to the defense of Washington—white men and black, the beaver hat alongside the carpenter's cap. We believed that Early's charge would sweep everything before it. But he did not charge! Oh, if it had been Jackson instead of Early! If it had been Gordon!—How the men cursed when Early withdrew!

One day in the latter part of July—the 23rd, I believe—625 of us were drawn up, amongst whom were Baxter, Atkinson, Adams, and myself. Under guard, we marched out of the front door to the R. R. station, elated with the hope that this removal might offer the chance of escape.

☆ **6** ☆

Elmira Prison

TRANSFERRED TO ELMIRA — PLANS FOR ESCAPE — LIFE IN A
YANKEE PRISON — THE TUNNELERS — ESCAPE FROM ELMIRA

☆ ☆ ☆ ☆ ☆ ☆ ☆ ☆ ☆ ☆ ☆

WE were put on board a train of freight cars, with a guard in each car—maybe two—and guards on top of the cars. I had made up my mind to seize the first chance I had to jump from the cars, but decided to wait for night decreasing the chance not only of being shot by the guards but also of re-capture.

In Baltimore, we were marched through the city. I remember very well passing by the Cathedral, along Cathedral St. While waiting in the depot, the citizens crowded upon us very close, looking at us with great interest, and, I thought, with sympathy. Once or twice my heart was in my mouth as a chance seemed about to be offered of slipping out amongst them, but the guards always drove them back too soon. During the journey, one of Mosby's men escaped, so I heard, by cutting a hole in the side of the car. The noise of the train prevented the guard from hearing, and other prisoners stood or sat around to hide him at his work. It was intended that others should follow, but the hole was discovered just after he had got out.

When night came on, I took a place by the door, and waited, hoping the guard would drop off to sleep. Then just when I had resolved to jump anyhow, the car shot past some large rocks many feet below in a ravine, on which I would have met instant death. And so, always deterred by one thing or another, I let the whole night go by. I certainly must have been unusually devoid of courage that night, and I have always been ashamed of it.

Reaching Elmira, Sunday, July 24th, we were marched through the streets to the outer edge of the town, where stood the prison, it being a camp like Point Lookout, with the same kind of wooden fence around it. Before getting inside the prison, I marked one object which seemed to promise a hope of escape. This was a large tree—I think a walnut—which grew in one corner, throwing its limbs out beyond the prison walls. Climbing it some dark night, one might go out on a limb and drop to the ground. Outside, near the entrance gate, were the guards' quarters—plain pine houses.

Inside, we were drawn up and the roll called, then assigned to our quarters, Baxter, Atkinson and I being assigned to the same long room with bunks fitted up on both sides, in two tiers. The bunks were made of unplaned pine boards, and as we had no blankets, they were left bare during the day, and at night occupied simply by ourselves. Later Baxter was given a blanket and a piece of cloth by a friend, and these he shared with me.

The prison was said to be a mile in circumference. In rear of it ran the Chemung (or Tioga) river, some 20 yards distant. Thro the middle of the prison, parallelling the river, lay a pool of water, probably 3 to 6 feet deep and about 40 feet wide. We were told that this was the old river bed, its course having been changed by a freshet. One end of the pool did not quite reach the fence; the other end ran under it, extending into the common beyond. Here a narrow bridge crossed the pool, a sentinel standing on it to keep anyone from going to the other side of the prison, at that time unoccupied.

The occupied part of the prison was, I believe, smaller than the other, the soil being hard, mixed with stones, while the unoccupied portion was low and sandy. When we arrived I think there were no tents, all prisoners then being lodged in the long wooden buildings. The sergeant of our ward was one of the guards, and we never saw him except at roll-calls (reveille and tattoo).

Shortly after our arrival, I came across Savage, Russell, Ferneyhough, and Johnson, whom I had left at Point Lookout. Russell had taken care of the things I had left at Point Lookout—my vest, shoes, etc.—and now he gave them to me; and he also paid a barber (a prisoner) to cut my hair, which had grown very long. Of course I had to tell them the whole of my history after leaving them, first making them promise not to repeat it to anyone, lest it reach the authorities, and so get me into trouble here at Elmira. I shortly met up with a member of my regiment, Sergt. Hood, who had been captured just a week after I was, by the very same troops, including the corporal who had pricked me with his bayonet. The corporal had shown him the knife with "Z. Benson" cut in the handle, which I had dropped during the struggle, and told him the story of my capture and attempt to escape.

Talking with Hood as to the prospect of escape, I now came to the conclusion that our best chance was to swim across the pool in the night, crawl along on our bellies to the fence and lying flat against it, dig a hole under it. The chief difficulty lay in being able to reach the fence, unobserved by the sentinel, and to remain unobserved while digging the hole. To minimize this danger, one should go first, leaving the others lying down at a distance, to be signaled by a stone thrown to them when the hole was dug. Baxter, Hood, Russell and I assembled one night to make the attempt. It being a bright, clear, starlit night we decided to wait for a darker night, preferably a stormy one. And the very next night, big locomotive lights were put all around inside the fence, so that the prison was like a gas-lit sidewalk.

I found here in prison an old schoolmate, John Perrin, who lived in a house in the north-east corner of the enclosure. With him was another Augusta boy, James Bohler. Between their house and the next one below it was a space only about three feet in width, making a long narrow alleyway, boarded up at both ends. I saw that if one were in this narrow alleyway, he could crawl under the adjoining house and start a tunnel, with little danger of being seen by anybody. So I proposed a plan to Perrin and Bohler, to which they agreed. They cut a little door in the side of their bunk, hinging it at the top with pieces of leather. To inquiring friends, they explained that this door was handy to spit out of when lying in their bunks smoking, or chewing tobacco. The first night after the door was completed, Perrin and I went out through it, and started a tunnel. We let in two or three others, to join in the attempt. After a few days, one of the newcomers took me aside saying he had something private to discuss with me. He told me that he belonged also to another gang of tunnelers, whose leaders asked me to visit them "on business." I went and was introduced to Joe Womack, a Confederate Sergeant Major. He proposed that we join forces and combine on one tunnel, saying that both tunnels could not succeed because at the first escape, a rigid search would be made, and the other inevitably discovered. Also, by combining forces, we could shorten the time of digging.

I was quite of the opinion of my new friends and promised them a coalition of forces. As their tunnel started from under one of the hospitals on the west side of the prison, and was much closer to the fence, we agreed to continue it and abandon ours. We had worked only three nights, when strange men were seen going in and out under the adjoining hospital, and we suspected that another tunnel was being dug under the adjoining hospital. Investigation the following night disclosed that tunnels were being dug from under all three hospitals. We sought out the leaders and held a council of war, at which it decided to abandon one of the three tunnels, continuing the other two. Both should be opened on the same night just as the sentinel on the fence called 11 o'clock.

The night agreed upon came (Aug. 28/64). Going early to the scene, I was surprised to see so many men about. There must have been scores lounging around—all talking about the tunnel and the prospect of its early completion. The chance of escape grew wonderfully small to me all at once. A few men might get out without discovery, but not scores! Determined to be one of the early ones, I went under. The ground under the building was almost covered with men lying down! Fearing that the attention of the guards would be attracted, and the men under the house captured, I crawled out, but continued to loiter nearby, chatting with a friend I had recently made, Jack Kibler, a Virginia cavalry scout. Directly men came streaming from under the house, making off, some of them at a run. A few words they let drop made the groups scattered about retire hastily too. Finally we halted one long enough for him to say, "The Yankees have found us out and driven stakes in the end of the tunnel."

I told Jack, "That isn't so. The Yankees wouldn't be so foolish as to stop the tunnel with stakes. They'd watch and catch the tunnelers. The leaders are just telling this tale to frighten the crowds away."

Jack agreeing with me, we crawled under the house. Two or three men were near the tunnel's mouth. When I asked whether anyone were in the tunnel, I was answered, "No." So off went my shoes, and I crawled in. Coming to the tunnel's end, I found solid dirt—no stakes. I backed out to the mouth and asked for a knife to dig with. A voice asked, "Is that you, Sullivan?"

"No," I answered. "Give me a knife."

They gave me one, and I set to work, working hard for some time, the air in the tunnel growing more and more foul as I breathed it over and over, until I was nearly suffocated, and had to come out for fresh air. I went back soon, taking a lighted candle someone gave me, and some matches. Soon the candle sputtered out and the matches refused to light. I kept working as long as I could stand it. When I came out again, someone took my place. So the work went on, by reliefs.

It had now grown late, probably 2 o'clock, Aug. 29th. Nearly everybody had gone, but I lay near the mouth of the tunnel, determined to stick it out to the end. After a while the tunneler came out and said he had opened the tunnel by a small hole, and found that it was just *inside* the wall. "Give me a tuft of grass to stop the hole up," he said.

The grass being given him, he crawled in to stop the hole, and came back saying, "The turf won't hold, but I pulled the grass over it, and I don't think it will be discovered."

There was some little talk between the two men as to completing the work the next night, neither aware of my presence within three feet of them, it was so dark. Then the man in the tunnel's mouth said to the other, "We'll go out tomorrow night if this is not found out. But if it is, why I've got another tunnel under way that was begun before this was thought of. I'll see you tomorrow."

"But," objected the other, "you don't know me by sight. We've never met except in the dark."

"Here," said the first voice, "you'll know me by this."

Nothing more being said, I crawled away, certain in my own mind that I knew exactly what was meant by "You'll know me by this," and just what action accompanied the words. Several times I had noticed a young man hanging around the hospital while the tunnel was being dug. Barefoot, dressed in a long gray jeans frock coat, sometimes reading or pretending to read, sometimes whittling, I had identified him in my mind as one of the other digging party. One thing that I noticed about him in particular was that the nail on the little finger of his left hand was an inch long. When I heard the words, "You'll know me by this," I was certain in my own mind that it was this man who put out his left hand to his companion, to feel the nail.

I crawled out and found it almost day, Aug. 29/64. After breakfast, I went to my bunk and turned in for a good long nap, telling Baxter to be ready for a long tramp that night. But some time during the day a friend came in and said, "Have you heard the bad news? The tunnel has been betrayed."

The commandant of Elmira Prison was Major Henry V. Colt, a brother of the Colt of pistol fame. Though our tunnels were broken up with pickaxes, and what workers could be found out, lodged in the guard-house, the commandant is reported to have said: "I must keep those fellows close, or they'll get away yet. If we hadn't caught them, they'd be halfway to Dixie by now. Well, I feel sorry for them, they deserved to succeed." This made us feel kindly toward him, realizing that he did not punish the men from cruelty, but merely to restrain them from a repetition of the attempt. The attendants at the guard-house honored the tunnelers with the title of the "Engineer Corps," and would not allow them to do any of the dirty work about the guard-house, making the criminals do it all.

Now that the old tunnel was broken up, I felt anxious to gain admittance into the one I had heard mentioned, and so began to look for my barefoot friend in the long coat and with the Chinese fingernail. But amidst several thousand people you can't find the man you want whenever you want him, and so my search for some time went unrewarded. Meanwhile daily life at Elmira followed a routine regular as clockwork. Roll call came first, then breakfast at eight. The menu too, followed a regular routine—so many days we had pork, so many days beef, so many days bean soup for dinner, so many days vegetable soup. The vegetable soup was made of a compound of several kinds of vegetables dried and pressed together in cakes resembling a plug of tobacco, not much liked by our men, the bean soup being much more popular. The "early settlers" reported that they had been served coffee at breakfast until on July 4th it was abruptly discontinued, no one knew why.

Since we couldn't be made to fight under the stars and stripes, we were made to eat under them, for along the joists above lay two immense flags that the boys cracked an infinite number of jokes about. The table furnishings were all of tin; the plates were shallow and didn't hold much soup. At first there were plenty of spoons, but the boys stole so many that a fellow was lucky to find a spoon alongside his plate, and many times we had to drink it from the sides of our plates. Sometimes soup would be left over in the kitchen, and then the officers would kindly announce that all who wanted extra soup might fall in line. The falling in was pretty general, it may be well believed. Once there was a line of men formed to go in, when, seeing in it a man I had something to say to, I walked up to him, not getting into the line, but simply standing alongside to speak to him, when an officer came up and ordering me off, struck me. Under this indignity, I had such feelings as never before in my life. To this day, I can hardly forgive myself for not striking back. I went straight to my quarters, trembling all over for a long time.

I have told how the men traded in crackers and tobacco at Point Lookout. At Elmira there was a regular market place where all the trading was done. I think it was the first day after my arrival that I was drawn thither by the sound of a fiddle, and there was a man playing away, with a crowd around him, on a fiddle which he had made of white pine (probably cracker boxes) and was now offering for sale. Here, too, the currency was tobacco, the value of a "ration" being a third of a plug. Since coffee was no longer served us, certain prisoners took to vending it. Having bought coffee, one would make a big boiler full and carry it around to sell—hot coffee, so much for a cracker, a cup full for so much tobacco cut off a plug. The place where this or anything else was cooked was the edge of the pool. Clever little fireplaces or "furnaces" as the men called them, were constructed, in which all the heat was so well utilized that a whole meal might be cooked of a single shingle split up fine. Shingles and bits of pine were obtained by begging the carpenters for waste when new buildings were going up. If not given away, it was stolen, which was just as satisfactory. To steal from prison authorities was considered a worthy exploit, but to steal from a comrade a man had to sink to the lowest depths of depravity.

When we first came, the water in the pool was clean; the men caught a good many fish there. But after a while the pool became so foul from the kitchen slops being thrown there that it began to stagnate and the authorities had some chemicals thrown in, which turned the water green and killed all the fish. Every morning the shore would be lined with the white bellies of dead fish.

I have said that the far side of the pool was low and

sandy; it was also covered with grass and weeds, and the men would sometimes go there and gather "lamb's quarter" or other such wild stuff as was known to be edible, of which there were a good many kinds that were known to those skilled in such craft.

Another item of fare which was not on the list furnished by the government was—rat! The prison swarmed with them—big rusty fellows which lived about the "cook house" as the kitchen was always called, and also under the houses used as quarters. The floors of these houses were close to the ground, and the sides came down all the way. The rats burrowed holes underneath to go in and out, sometimes as large as a man's leg. Down on the bank of the Pool they burrowed great holes extending far under ground. It was a usual sight at dusk, when the rats would be scampering about, to see men down on the bank with stones watching for a rat to come out, and when he appeared, such a hurrah and such a chase and such a volley of stones! You would have thought it was our Battalion of Sharpshooters in a charge. Most of the boys followed this kind of chase for excitement. But I think there is little doubt of the truth of the stories told that some broiled and ate them.

Among the prisoners was one named Williams who had a little dog, a terrier, and the two together made an unceasing war upon rats. The dog, of course, was worth his weight in - - I can't say gold; I must say tobacco—and the spoils of the chase kept him well fed. Once Williams was arrested for prowling around camp in the middle of the night. Taken to Headquarters next morning, he was asked by the Major, "What were you doing?"

"Huntin', sir."

"*What* were you hunting?"

"Rats."

Inquiring further, the major was told that the rats were fed to the dog, the skins sold to make gloves, and that the nightly catch was usually a dozen or more. After thinking a moment, the major called a sergeant and instructed: "Ser-

geant, have this man detailed on special duty—to catch rats.
Have double rations issued to him—one for himself and one
for his dog." Turning to the prisoner, he continued, "Now
Williams, do you report to me every morning with the rats
you have caught."

After that, every morning, Williams was seen at headquarters with a string of rats in his hand—or so the story was
told to me.

Our drinking water came from wells, into which the rats
used to fall and drown, the water becoming so unbearable
that somebody would have to go down and clean out; it
seemed to me that we were always cleaning out the wells.

There was a strange character in the prison who went
by the name of Buttons. A large man, he wore a large grey
frock coat with rather long tails, which at a distance looked
like a veritable coat of mail. For this coat was literally
covered with brass buttons, hundreds of them, so that in
the sunshine he fairly glistened. Where he got the buttons
to gratify his strange taste, I never heard; and I never heard
him called by any other name than "Buttons." It was generally true that whenever soldiers could hit upon a nickname
which was in any way characteristic, that name would take
preference over the legitimate one. Examples are: "Gator" of
Co. H.; Munnerlyn who was always called "Old Son";
Rothwell who was called "Promptly"; Peagler, invariably
addressed as *Mister* Peagler; and a Scotchman named Smythe,
who was dubbed "City of Glasgow." In prison, where there
were men from all sections, the most frequent nick-name was
that of one's state. At Elmira I was called "South C'lina" more
often than "Benson."

The prison kept growing in population till there were said
to be 10,000—quite a little city in itself. Tents were set up
on the far side of the pool and occupied as quarters, and free
passage was allowed between the sections except at night.
Amongst so many prisoners deaths were necessarily frequent,
and at one time the mortality rate was pretty bad. It was
reported amongst us that one of the Federal surgeons said

this excessive mortality was the result of insufficient food—
that we got enough to sustain life, but not enough to resist
disease. Personally I never believed that a Federal surgeon
said this.

One day a number of prisoners were brought in, and as
usual we crowded around to see if any friends were amongst
them. I noticed a prisoner standing apart, who appeared to be
under special guard, and so he proved to be. He had attempted
to escape on the route, and now was to be punished by close
confinement. While close confinement may have been war-
ranted, the abuse I now saw heaped upon him by some of
the officers certainly was not. He was treated as though he
had done something mean and criminal. This man was a sort
of lay preacher. He was called insulting names, and even told
that his attempt to escape was inconsistent with his profession
of religion, as though to remain a captive when caught were
a sacred duty. There were a good many preachers in prison;
we used to have preaching every Sunday and sometimes
oftener; and there were constant prayer meetings in various
parts of the camp. Once a brother of Henry Ward Beecher
came to preach to us, and afterwards for a time he returned
on every third Sunday.

During this time I considered various plans of escape, even
trying to figure how I might go out in the covered wagon
that drove out daily with the dead. Most of all, I continued
to look for my fellow workman of that eventful night in
the destroyed tunnel, him of the Chinese finger-nail. I haunted
all sorts of places, preachings and prayer meetings, the market—any place where numbers of men gathered together. I
even staid about outside the dining rooms during meal hours,
inspecting the various wards as they marched in. Finally one
morning early I was strolling down by the Pool when my
eyes fell on the familiar long frock coat, and the figure
of the man I sought.

He strode deliberately and unconcernedly down to the
edge of the Pool and there took a seat, I watching him. He
put his hand in his coat pocket, and taking out something,

dropped it gently in the water at his feet. The motion was repeated. Then again and again. But I did not need even the second movement to know exactly what he was doing. He was getting rid of stones that he had dug out of his tunnel! I felt alarm lest amongst the men standing around, there might be someone sharp enough to divine the meaning of his actions— some oath-taker maybe, who would betray him.

I walked down to him, when seeing me approach, he stopped his work and folded his arms across his knees. I said quietly, "You'd better be careful; some fellow may see you and tell on you."

"Tell what? I'm not doing anything!"

"I saw you putting stones in the water."

"Well, there's no harm in that, is there?"

"No, if you were not digging a tunnel. No man would take such pains to dispose of a few stones if he were not digging a tunnel. Here, I'll stand between you and the crowd. Empty your pockets."

Without another word, he got rid of all his stones; then rising said, "Walk with me a little way."

When we were away from the crowd, he said, "Yes, I am digging a tunnel. There is a party of us, and we're bound by oath not to even hint of it to the dearest friend. But since you've found out without my telling you, I've no doubt that if you want to join us, the boys will be glad enough to take you in. We need another good hand."

I told him that was exactly what I wanted, adding that I had been with him in the other tunnel tho' he did not know it. He then appointed a time and place of meeting— the 3rd tent from the end in the 2nd row from the wall. Arriving at the appointed time, I found in the tent a little party of four or five—all strangers. Introduced by my Alabama friend, whose name was Traweek, we shook hands all around. When all had assented to my becoming a member, a Testament was brought, and with my hand upon it, I took solemn oath not to divulge by word or sign the existence of the party or its operations. In order to avoid disputes as to precedence, it was a law of the group that the men should go out of the tunnel, upon its completion, in the order in which they had been admitted to the society. There were nine before me in the group, of which several were not present. As the tenth man, I felt that my chances of escape would not be great, for I believed that not more than three or four were likely to get away without discovery. Still, there was a chance, and I determined to go to work with all my energy, not neglecting meanwhile any other opportunity that might offer.

The oath being taken, a blanket was turned back from the bed, the dried grass used for a bed scraped away, two short pieces of plank taken up, and the mouth of the tunnel revealed. It was a pit about waist deep and between 2 and 2½ feet square. At the bottom on the side nearest the fence was the beginning of the tunnel proper. The tent from which it started was near the north-east corner of the prison, and the distance to the fence or wall was roughly estimated as between 50 and 60 feet. One line of tents being between it and the fence, we would have to pass under one tent. At the time I joined, the tunnel had attained a length of about 15 feet. Its entrance was a great improvement on that of the one I had started, for I had begun mine by slanting it down to the proper depth, and it was hard to back out of it. But as this one began with a perpendicular shaft, all one had to do was to straighten himself up when he got in the shaft.

I now set to work in good earnest. It might be supposed that night was the best time for this work, but seldom was anything done after nine at night, the dangers of detection being greater after silence had settled over the prison. Our best time was between sundown and eight o'clock when activity was at its peak, and actually a good deal of digging went on during the day. Luckily the sergeant of our ward was a Confederate and moreover he was one of us. He would always announce to us when inspection was to take place. But sometimes we had to wait two or three days before the officers finally came, and during that time nothing could be done, for fear of discovery.

One great trouble was disposing of the dirt and stones taken from the tunnel. Sometimes one of the men would venture on taking out a haversack full of dirt under a big coat. But the usual means was in little sacks we had made to fit into our pockets. Some of this was emptied into the sinks, some into the rat holes, while the bank of a new ditch being dug was regarded as a splendid place. Once during a rain at night we strewed dirt along the street, expecting the rain to obliterate all traces. It did well enough to escape general observation, but we could detect it next morning, and were uneasy.

The stones, except for the biggest ones, were an easier matter. A few large ones we had to sneak out with after dark and drop them quietly in the pool. I'm not sure but that some of the biggest were buried in the tent. The smaller stones were easy to get rid of. I would fill my coat pockets with them and taking a book, which I pretended to read, sit down with my back against one of the buildings where the floor came nearly to the ground and with a twitch of my hand send a stone far back under the building. One building was a favorite of mine until finally I had thrown so many stones under that house that I could not throw another without hearing it hit some stone that had gone before. A favorite place to deposit stones was in the rat holes. I would sit by a rat hole and drop the stones in until I could see the top stones, then move to another hole. The next day it could be filled again, for in the night the rats would move all the stones away in order to get in and out of their hole. Then when in the dusk the rats were running about, the men after them with stones, we would fill our pockets and join in the chase. There was no such lavish expenditure of ammunition amongst other hunters as with us. All our stones, moreover, were so thrown as to bounce eventually into the Pool, lest their fresh, earthy look might next day excite suspicion. And we did not at all need to see a *real* rat. In the dusk an imaginary one might be chased, with cries of, "Here he goes—Kill him!" and a terrific bombardment of stones. Outsiders coming up to join the chase never guessed that there was no rat, but thought simply that he had got away.

That was the way the stuff was disposed of; the tunneling itself was harder. The blankets and dried grass having been removed and the planks taken up, you got into the shaft. Then on hands and knees you crawled into the tunnel and lay flat. Beyond the first body-length, the tunnel decreased in size until it was only large enough to admit the body, and in some places it was a squeeze at that. Thus only the toes and the points of the elbows were used in propelling yourself forward. Having got to the end of the tunnel, your body blocking the way behind, and leaving the least bit of air in front to breathe, you fell to with a butcher knife, one of a supply the boys had managed to steal from the cook house. In less than a minute you were panting like a dog—for air. A minute was enough to give one the most violent, racking headache, and you knew perfectly well in entering the tunnel that you had this to expect.

When the digger had loosened so much of dirt and stones as to incommode him, he laid down his knife and crawled backward, scooping the earth back with his hands and arms until he had carried it about the length of his body. Then he crawled forward and resumed his digging, by now fighting against suffocation. An assistant crawled in behind him and removed the dirt to the tunnel's mouth, scooping it along with his hands and arms as he inched himself laboriously backward. When the man at the end could stand the suffocation no longer, his head seeming about to burst with pain, his tongue thrust out, breathing fast to keep his blood supplied with the poisoned air, he called to the man behind him to "back out," and both backed to the shaft, and a fresh couple went in.

To keep our clothes from getting so covered with fresh dirt as to attract attention, those of us who managed to secure an extra shirt and trousers or drawers, kept them especially for excavation. But those of us who could secure no change of clothes turned our clothes wrong side out to go into the tunnel. Traweek was the best tunneler in the party, and I was generally accounted second best, this being gauged by what we could accomplish under the suffocating conditions which we must endure. One of our best workmen, Fox Maull, had to give up work in the tunnel entirely, being seized with nausea and violent vomiting, from breathing the poisoned air. But he made up for it by zeal at other tasks.

Being bound by oath, I could not say a word to Baxter; but from a few things he let drop, I inferred that he attributed my prolonged absences to the right cause. Nor could I hint of it to my friends Adams and Atkinson, both of whom were most generous in sharing with me gifts they received from some friends they had in the north. When I coveted a pocket compass on sale in the camp for 30cts, Adams bought it and presented it to me, and I could not tell him the use I hoped to make of it. He also told me the name and address of a lady in Baltimore who had befriended him, and I stored it in my mind, thinking it might be useful if I found myself a fugitive in that city.

A new friend I had made in the prison was Jack Kibler, a cavalryman from Virginia, whose hardihood, strength, and knowledge of the border country would have made him an ideal companion in an attempt to escape, and he was as bent upon escape as I was. I fell in with a plan of his for scaling the wall with a ladder, helping him to steal lumber, and make the ladder, which, in sections, he hid under his bed. Being extremely doubtful that fugitives from the tunnel could escape detection so far as the tenth man, I was ready to participate in alternate plans which might prove feasible.

But the tunnel continued undiscovered so long that we grew more and more hopeful every day, and worked harder than ever. Dirt went out by the haversackful, and stones by the score. With the prospect of early completion, I determined that for the present I would do nothing in any other direction, but bend all my efforts toward the completion of the tunnel.

The length of the tunnel was measured with a string and compared with the estimated distance from its mouth to the fence, and it was found that we ought to be within three feet of the fence. But as we worked at the end of the tunnel, the footsteps of the guards passing on their rounds just inside the fence did not appear to pass overhead but some distance away. We held a conclave and I proposed that one of us should go to the end of the tunnel and listen to blows which on some pretext should be struck on the ground. So a piece of tin was procured, and a piece cut off in rough imitation of a spoon. About four of us took this out on the grass about where we thought the end of the tunnel should be. Sitting down, one began hammering away on the tin, using one stone as a hammer, another as anvil, making all the noise possible, for the benefit of the listener in the tunnel. If the sentinel on the fence heard us talking about "making a spoon" and "bringing it into shape" he paid little attention, for he had seen Johnny Reb hammering out a tin spoon before.

Directly a man came from the tent and joining us quietly said, "He says you're too far to the left."

We shifted position to the right and commenced hammering again.

Presently came another man strolling from the tent, who sat down casually, took the spoon and looked at it, with the remark, "He says you're *still* too far to the left."

Watching till the two nearest sentries turned their backs, we shifted again, further to the right, and again commenced hammering. Directly we saw the man from inside the tunnel standing unconcernedly outside the tent door. Leaving our stones to mark the spot, we adjourned with our spoon, such as it was. When the tunneler declared that the last knocking had been right over his head, we felt sure that he must be somehow mistaken. But we dared not repeat the experiment right away, lest so much activity excite suspicion.

Then a thought struck me and I said, "Let's run a little hole up through the roof from the end of the tunnel. I know where to get a ramrod, and the small hole it will make won't be noticed."

The men agreeing, I went in search of a man I'd seen that morning with an iron ramrod. With this heated red-hot, he had been hollowing out a hole in a walking stick he'd made. Guessing his purpose, I had said, "Going to send a letter home, aren't you?"

Looking up surprised he said, "No. Why do you think so?"

"You're boring that hole to put a letter in, and you'll give the stick to a friend in that batch of prisoners they're making up for exchange. You don't want Major Holt reading your letter—that's all." The man still looking at me in surprise, I added, "Don't be afraid of my telling on you. I'm no oath taker."

I found my man easily, and he lent me his ramrod willingly, grateful that I had not told on him. While a man inside the tunnel worked the ramrod slowly up to the surface, several stood around talking, about where we expected it to come up. Directly one made a step forward, putting his foot on the end of the ramrod as it came through a tuft of grass very close to the stones with which we had marked this spot. We now knew exactly where we were. But what a crook in the tunnel this indicated! We were about 10 feet off from a straight line drawn from the tunnel's mouth to the fence.

After talking it over we came to the conclusion that the curve in our tunnel was due to right-handedness. To get the proper use of his right hand, the digger had to lie on his left side. The tendency was thus always to work a little to the front, and the tunnel continually inclined to the right. Someone now suggested that the aperture made by the ramrod be enlarged a little, thus obtaining for the diggers a supply of fresh air, which was increasingly needed as the tunnel grew in length. So we widened the tunnel a little at this point, and dug away some of the dirt overhead, making a little chamber in which a man could sit hunched, his knees drawn up to his chin. Then we enlarged the ramrod hole to about the size of three fingers, and the "Ventilator" was made. When we worked at night the hole in the surface was left open, without fear of discovery. In the day, two or three men would sit around reading, talking, or playing mumble peg, ready to cover it if need arose. When we were not at work, a stone was laid over it.

One day an order came from Major Colt for Traweek to report at headquarters. Supposing that he had got a "money-letter" or a box from home, we awaited his return without alarm. We waited and waited, but he did not return. Finally the Orderly Sergeant, who as I have said, was of our party, went to inquire. He came back with the dreadful news that Traweek was not only in the guardhouse, but locked up in a cell! This had only one meaning for us—our plot was discovered, we would all be arrested and lodged in cells, escape farther away than ever. As the moments slipped by, we wondered why we were not arrested.

At dinner time, the Orderly carried Traweek his dinner, and Traweek told him what had happened. Talking with some friends, Traweek had unwisely bragged about his part in digging the other tunnels, the ones from the hospital that had been destroyed. An oath taker, overhearing his remarks, had reported him. It was a great relief to know that our tunnel was safe. But how about Traweek? He had been the originator and moving spirit of this enterprise, and all agreed that we could not desert him. I don't know just how it was managed, but tools were secured and smuggled in to him, and Traweek managed to loosen the planks across the top of his cell so that they could be removed at any time. Through the opening thus made, he could reach the loft, whence through a back window he could let himself down to the ground. We would send him word when the tunnel was ready and he would escape from his cell that night and join us.

Major Colt had questioned Traweek as to his confederates in the hospital tunnel, but Traweek had declared that he didn't know a soul. He finally admitted under pressure that he did know one man named Jim, but insisted that he knew neither his other name, nor his ward. The Major finally said, "Very well, I'll lock you in a cell until you find this Jim." Every now and then the Major would drop by the guardhouse, have Traweek brought out, and ask him in a joking kind of way, "Well, have you found Jim yet?" knowing full well that "Jim" was a Johnny Reb born of Traweek's imagination. And

Traweek would laugh too and answer, "No sir, Major, not yet."

Finally the Major, out of the goodness of his heart, sent Traweek word that he would release him if he would give his word of honor not to try to escape from prison again. Traweek sent back word that he thanked him but could not in justice to himself make such a promise, for if an opportunity to escape should present itself, he would feel bound to take advantage of it. To this, the Major is said to have replied, "Oh, very well! There's no other tunnel going on that I'm aware of, and it's hardly probable that you'll break down the fence." (How we tunnelers chuckled over this, for at that very moment our tunnel was near completion, and we had a little army prepared with a ladder ready, if not to break down the fence, at any rate to climb over it.)

After we had progressed a little way beyond the Ventilator, we experienced the same suffocation while digging as we had before. But the Ventilator caused some change and improvement in the way of working. The digger still hauled the dirt as before to the one behind him. But the dirt-remover now staid huddled in the ventilator, getting fresh air, until signaled. He still must rake the dirt with hands and arms as far as the ventilator, but there he deposited it in a small wooden box which had two long, strong cords fastened to it, one at each end. He then gave a rap on the box as a signal, a man in the tent pulled it in, the man at the ventilator letting his cord slip thro' his hands. The passage of the box, however, was never made smoothly; it was always catching on some projecting rock and having to be pulled back a little way and given a fresh start.

So, besides those who kept going in and out of the tent, disposing of dirt and stones, the work took four men—one to dig, one in the ventilator, one in the shaft, and one to stand at the door and keep anybody from coming in. For any friend would have just parted the flaps of the tent and walked right in, if no one had been at the entrance to prevent. Coming to pay a visit, such a friend would be told, "Don't go in right now; Traweek's washing all over" or "Don't go in now; Maull is dressing." Such visitors must have thought these dwellers in tents to have been a remarkably modest set of men.

It was now early in October. On Wednesday, Oct. 5th we knew by measurement that we were close to the fence, and our ears confirmed this, for we could hear the guards tramp right over our heads as they walked their beat just inside the fence. We worked steadily on the 5th and 6th, fixing the time for our escape at 10 o'clock the night of the 6th. Our Orderly Sergeant, who did no work inside the tunnel on account of a wounded arm, but had been invaluable in other ways, now decided not to go with us. Besides being handicapped by his wound, he had been given reason to hope for an early exchange, along with some other sick and wounded. This would advance me to 9th place instead of 10th. Looking north towards the mountains, we could see a broad highway winding among the fields. Some of the men said, "That leads to Canada; that's the road I'm going to take." As for me, I had no other thought nor wish than to go south and re-join Lee's army.

On the 6th I got everything ready: 2 pocket knives; half of a kit to cook in; a few matches; my penciled map; my pocket compass; and some strong cord to serve as a bridle if I could steal a horse. We fixed a point of woods in the mountain to meet and have a last talk and final goodbye. Most of the men were going in couples. I was again going alone.

As it grew dark we prepared for action. No dirt was to be carried outside tonight; it was to be left in the tent. Traweek took first turn at the digging, I in the Ventilator. Being the fastest workers, we were to do the remainder of the digging. But there was more work to be done than had been expected. At 10 o'clock we had not yet reached the fence. About that time a heavy storm passed over— just the thing for an escape! It looked as though Fate had made an appointment with us and we had failed to come to time.

In the tunnel the knife plugged away steadily, the box slid

back and forth with its load of dirt. Traweek would stand the suffocation as long as he could, then we must both back out all the way to the tent and change places, I going in first to take my turn. In the tent was an eager listening to the faint sounds from the tunnel, low whispers, a grasp on a fellow's arm at any sound from without. In all hearts were hope, fear, and anxiety, as the box slid back and forth and the knife pegged away.

I became wretchedly sick, with a violent headache and nausea, and so did Traweek. Once as I crawled back to the ventilator, the roof of the tunnel broke in, quantities of dirt and stone falling on my legs. But as no rush of fresh air followed, I knew that the surface had not broken. I called quietly to the shaftsman, who came and removed the dirt. This consumed much time. It was now past midnight.

Once as I occupied the ventilator, I worked my hand up and widened the hole a little, to admit more air. This could do no harm now, it being the last night. Traweek called, "Benson, let's change; I can't stand it any longer."

This time, instead of inching slowly backwards the length of the tunnel, I squeezed my back against one side of the ventilator, saying, "Traweek, see if we can't pass one another here." Down he came slowly, first his feet in my face, then further and further, while I jammed myself against the side of the tunnel. Now we were face to face. I tried to move forward, but could not. He tried to move down, and he could not. We could move neither way—we were wedged! We had begun to think we had made an end of it, when a desperate effort set us free, and I went to digging, he to the Ventilator.

And now as I plied the knife, my head seemed on the point of bursting. My mouth wide open, tongue protruding, panting like a dog, I felt the lack of breath not in my lungs only, but in my whole body. With every beat of my heart, great throbs of pain coursed through me. Having stood it as long as I could, I was relieved by Traweek, we passing one another more easily at the Ventilator this time.

When he next called for relief, Traweek told me that he had struck a big rock which projected downward from the roof of the tunnel. He was afraid to use force against it, as it might break the surface. I found it as he said, and very much in the way. After feeling all round it carefully, I gave a quick wrench and it fell, *broken in two*, the upper part remaining in the roof. During his next turn at digging Traweek called softly, "Benson, I've struck a fence post!"

"Good!" I whispered back, for this meant that our digging was near an end. Taking my turn, I worked to the right around the post, until I knew the end of the tunnel was outside the fence. Feeling that I was dying for air, I reached up my hand and worked it through the pebbly soil, which came raining down in my face—my eyes shut, for of what use are eyes in a tunnel? I felt cold air on my fingers, and withdrew my arm, the cold stream following. I lay on my back, enjoying that feast of air, that luxury of breath. Then I crawled back and sent Traweek up to get his share of it.

Pretty soon we had hollowed out all but a thin shell on top, and our last 'work was to dig a hole under that for the dirt to drop into when the break was made. Then Traweek and I went out and announced that the tunnel was ready, and the boys began gathering up what they needed to take with them, I slipping to my quarters to get coat and shoes. Baxter was awake, late though it was. Because of my oath, I could only say something unimportant, and with a sad heart leave him, not even saying goodbye.

Back in the tent, the exit had not yet begun, and as the departures were to be made at considerable intervals, it would take some time. So I lay down, to get some ease for my head, which almost crazed me. Directly I fell into a sort of a doze, only half conscious of what was going on in the tent. I was suffering such pain in my head that I didn't much care whether I went or stayed. In this half conscious state I heard someone say, "They are still working in the tunnel."

I started to my feet. It was Shelton speaking; only he, the seventh man, and his companion, the eighth, remained in the tent. He said that he had been down in the tunnel and had heard those who had gone before, down at the end working. When I protested that this could not be the case, since Traweek and I had finished the tunnel, he still believed that he had heard the men inside.

I said, "Let me go in then, I'll find out."

He agreed, saying, "If you find the way clear, call back to us."

Having crawled nearly to the ventilator, I knew that six men could not be stowed in the remainder of the tunnel, so I called back to Shelton to come on. In a few minutes I was at the outer mouth of the tunnel, finding all open, above me the platform running around outside the fence. I raised my head and looked out. On the other side of the street stood three sentinels with rifles, around a fire. I crawled out and wormed my way along under the platform, close to the fence, towards the town. After a little, I got on hands and knees and went faster, the sentinel tramping along above my head. When I had got a tree between me and the three sentinels, I rose to my feet and walked rapidly along under the platform to the corner of the prison. What I had now to do was full of risk. I had to step out from under the platform in full view of the sentinels on it. At a brisk pace, but not hurrying, I stepped out and crossed the street diagonally, not turning my head, though I felt every moment that I would hear a shot and feel a bullet pierce my back. But there was no shot and no challenge. Reaching the other side of the street, I walked quickly down the pavement for about forty yards. Then fearing I might meet some sentinel or patrol, I jumped into a front yard, and ran into the back yard and then into a vegetable garden, when a big dog made at me. I jumped the back fence into a lane, and away I fled toward the mountain.

I ran until exhausted, then stopped and looked back. There lay the prison under its bright lights, white with tents, populous with a sleeping multitude. And there were the pickets, the blind pickets, calmly walking their beats. Is it to be wondered at that I should give vent to my joy in unseemly ways, jumping up and cracking my heels together, throwing my hat in the air? As I made my way to the point of woods where we had engaged to meet, it was all I could do to keep from shouting "The Bonnie Blue Flag" at the top of my voice.

☆ 7 ☆

A Fugitive in Enemy Country

WANDERINGS IN THE MOUNTAINS — FORAGING FOR A LIVING —
DOWN THE SUSQUEHANNA — RIDING THE TRAINS — DISAPPOINT-
MENT IN BALTIMORE — TO THE POTOMAC — SWIMMING THE
POTOMAC AGAIN — HOME TERRITORY — MOSBY'S MEN —
REUNITED WITH BLACKWOOD

☆ ☆ ☆ ☆ ☆ ☆ ☆ ☆ ☆ ☆ ☆

AT the appointed meeting place I gave the signal, getting
no answer. I called Traweek and Fox Maull by name. No
reply. Then as daylight slowly spread its first signs over the
hills and valleys, and over the white camp of captive soldiers,
I turned to the forest. It was now morning of the 7th of
October, 1864.

Passing thro' a cornfield, I put some of the ears in my
pockets. Then I came to an orchard, and oh how delicious
the apples were! I filled my pockets and ate as I went on,
half walking, half running. After a while I got into a road
running westward. This must be my course for a time, following up the river, for I feared to cross a bridge anywhere
near the prison, lest it might be guarded.

Coming in sight of a house, I saw a man in the yard, and
as I could not pass without being seen, I turned off the road
and climbed up the mountain at my right. It was so steep
that I had to pull myself up by the bushes. Near the top of
the mountain, I came to a precipitous rock about 40 feet high.
At the foot of this I rested a while. But anxious to conceal
myself better, I resumed my climb. With the aid of slight

151

footholds on projecting rocks, and scraggy bushes here and there, I clambered half way up and got into a niche in the rock, whence I could see the country for miles around.

Far below lay the house I had avoided and the river rolling by, spanned by a bridge—Fitch Bridge, no doubt. Beyond the valley were other hills, clothed with field and forest and orchard, dotted with farmhouses. It was a beautiful picture, and best of all, Elmira was no longer in sight. But as it was now near sunrise I lay and listened for the morning gun, and laughed to think how when the Union Sergeant called the roll at reveille, he would call, "Benjamin Benson, Benjamin Benson!" and then look up and say, "Where is Benjamin Benson?" For both at Old Capitol and Elmira, they wrote "Berry" as I told them and then couldn't read their own writing and took it for "Benj." But the sun rose and I did not hear the morning gun, I was too far away. The rocks about were filled with the prints of seashells that lived when not only the deep valley before me, but the heights upon which I lay were the bed of the ocean.

I staid here a part of the day, and then moved more into the forest and lay down on the wet leaves and tried to sleep, but I could not. I wanted to sleep so as to travel all the following night, but my excitement and anxiety were too great to allow sleep, tho' I had been awake all the night before. So I went on down the mountain, thro' the forest, westward, and crossed a deep ravine, thro' which flowed a cold, clear brook, over and amongst great boulders which had rolled down the mountainside, meeting at the bottom in this ravine. After washing my face and hands in the brook, I climbed half way up the opposite mountain, then lay down on the wet leaves and ate some of my apples. I dared not make a fire yet to parch my corn. I think I slept a little here; but soon I was up again continuing my climb over this second mountain.

About dark I went down to an orchard, where I saw some children gathering apples. Waiting hidden till they were gone, I went in and filled my pockets again. Such a treat as these apples were after a long summer without fruit or even fresh vegetables. If I remember right I had during my prison life, two apples and a peach. I think they were given me by Adams, who received them from his northern friends.

To travel by night over the mountains was impracticable, so as soon as it was dark (10/7) I took the high road, still leading west. I stopped at some walnut trees and ate a few. Then coming to a school house on the right of the road, I managed to raise one of the windows and enter, in the hope that some pretty young girl had left half her lunch. Finding no food, I climbed out again, disappointed. It was a dark cloudy night, and I wished it would rain, which would make it even better for a fugitive. By striking matches and looking at my compass, I could tell directions. Though my map was only a rough pencil sketch of the important points in a narrow belt of country over which I expected to pass, it was serviceable. As soon as I could safely cross the river, I intended to head south for Baltimore, then go west to Leesburg, to my friend, Judge Gray. After that I would be guided by circumstances.

It must have been about 9 P.M. (10/7) when I passed through a town which I presume was Big Flats, though I had no means of learning its name for certain. It began to rain, and I crept into a tobacco house "of Col. Barney Hoffman," according to a sign, and slept for a while in an empty box, then traveled on. I have never been able fully to understand this night's journey. I remember going down to the river once (on a small road, I think) but finding no bridge, I kept on, my road lying between the river on my left, and the railroad on my right. It must have been this night that I crossed the river on a bridge—I don't remember whether it was a railroad bridge or not. There was a little sort of hamlet on the near side, a town on the far side. I suppose the former was Knoxville, the latter Corning.

I was walking along a lane that led South when I heard the sound of chickens in an apple tree close by. I climbed over a fence, and reaching up, touched feathers, when out flew a big rooster, and I gave chase. When finally my hand closed on him, he slipped through a crack in the fence, and I was left with a handful of feathers. I got among mountains again, and at daylight Oct. 8th, I stopped at some distance from the road, on the side of a steep hill where I made a little fire and parched some of my corn, and ate some apples. Apples I could get almost anywhere, by jumping over a fence into an orchard and taking my pick.

That night, Saturday, Oct. 8th, I struck camp and continued South. It was getting very cold, and my coat was only the thin, summer coat that I had swapped for in July in the Old Capitol. Soon it began to snow. I trudged on, taking the snow and the wind, eating apples, for I had nothing else to eat. But it grew worse, finally becoming so cold that I was obliged to take shelter in a barn which stood to the left of the road. Crawling into the hay, I slept for a while. When the snow stopped, I got up, gathered up my apples, which had rolled out of my pockets into the hay, and plodded on. Just before day, I passed thro' a little village. Determined to make a raid for some kind of food, I went into the premises of one of the houses, and found a chicken roost. I reached up and grabbed a chicken by the neck, squeezing so hard it couldn't make a sound, then cut its head off with my knife. Buttoning the chicken under my coat, I then made time.

At good daylight, I passed a little schoolhouse where was an Irish potato patch. I grabbled some of these and also picked up a few chestnuts under a tree close by. Then I went off to the mountains and built a fire and broiled my chicken and roasted some of the potatoes—the first food aside from a handful of parched corn and plenty of apples that I had had for two days and three nights. Meanwhile I had drunk no water, the apples serving for both food and drink. After eating the chicken, I was thirsty for the first time since leaving prison, and I drank from a little spring close by. I suppose I was now in Pennsylvania, a few miles South of the State Line and about southwest from Elmira.

Sometime during the night of Oct. 9th, I came to a railroad and decided to follow the tracks. I don't know what time of night it was when I came to a fork and took the left, a creek running along by the side of the railroad on the right— probably Tioga River. As I traveled up stream, the railroad turned more and more to the left, and it seemed to be going up the mountain. After I had gone a mile or more, I found I was going due north. Deciding that this must be a spur line, leading probably to a coal mine, I turned round and went back to the fork and took the right hand branch of the railroad. I kept plodding on all that night, and just at dawn (Oct. 10th) I was brought to an astounded standstill by finding the road to *end* right in a swamp. There was no depot, no station house, no house of any kind—just swamp!

On a hillside not far from the railroad's abrupt ending I found a little village—one long street with cottages on both sides, all built alike. Now and then I met men, all dressed in black, each carrying a tin bucket in his hand, and a piece of candle stuck in his hat. I knew then a coal mine must be nearby, and these were miners going to work. None of them seemed to pay any attention to me, for which I was glad. Getting out of the village as soon as possible, I found a secluded spot in the woods where I camped for the day.

It was a queer place I was in. Although it was high in the hills, it was so swampy that I could not find a dry place to lie down. Great masses of rocks lay amongst the mud and moss. I think I had nothing to eat but a little parched corn, tho' I may have had a few apples. But I remained there until darkness fell, Monday, Oct. 10th.

Tired of getting tangled up in mountains and rivers and railroads that ran in circles and then dumped one off in a swamp, I determined to ask the road to Canton, at the first opportunity. Not that I wanted particularly to go to Canton, which I remembered as a railroad station we had passed through on the way to Elmira, but at least if I got there, I would know where I was. So I went back to the village and knocked on the door of the last house, which was convenient to the woods, where I could make a run for it, if I were met with suspicion.

The lady who answered my knock, gave directions for going to Canton, saying the distance was nine miles. Then a man's voice from inside inquired how I happened to be going to Canton tonight. I answered with my now familiar story of search for a stray horse. The man said that I must be tired, that I'd better come in and have a cup of tea! Deciding to risk it, I entered and found him lying on a bed in an adjoining room. I was invited to sit down and was served not only tea but supper. As I consumed everything but the dishes, the man asked fifty questions, to which, perforce, I answered fifty lies. Every once in a while he would say, "If you'd come a little sooner, you'd have got something better than tea." He told me he was a Scotchman, and that his name was Adams. I forget what my name was at the time—probably Jefferson. When he had given me clear instructions as to the route, we two presidents parted. Bless his old soul, if I'd told him I was an escaped prisoner from Elmira, he'd have insisted on my hiding under his bed. He had just enough of what he called "something-better-than-tea" inside him to make him do it.

It was just 9 o'clock by his watch when I left the affable Scot. At daybreak Tuesday, Oct. 11th, I reached the railroad, three miles above Canton! I had spent the intervening time plodding away, following directions as faithfully as I could, but somehow still lacked three of the nine miles I was supposed to travel. And four days out, I was just 35 miles South of Elmira, when I ought to have been a hundred. I went off to a piece of woods on the right of the road and camped in a sort of sink in the ground, and if I am not mistaken I had broiled chicken for breakfast.

It must have been near Fall Brook that I went into a back yard and abstracted some clothes from the bannisters—stockings and trousers, I think. I put the trousers on under my own in an effort to keep warm. When next I pulled them off, I found my legs were black with coaldust. The trousers had been airing, instead of drying after being washed.

At dusk Oct. 11th, after an all day's rest, I started briskly down the railroad, soon passing Canton—the first familiar landmark. It was now 40 miles to Williamsport on the west branch of the Susquehanna; and it would take me two nights to get there. I trudged on, shivering with cold. About 7 miles past Canton a little cabin stood close to the railroad tracks. In a square hole cut in the side of the cabin for a window, I saw something dark. Going up and feeling it, I found it to be rough, heavy cloth—what if it were a coat? I began pulling at it, and though I could hear someone inside the house snoring, I kept pulling until it was outside in my hands. It was a famous warm overcoat that I had captured, just when I sorely needed it. And the pockets—there were four of them! And it was all the more in keeping with my appearance that it was somewhat ragged and worn.

The road now went skirting along the side of a mountain which towered up on my left, and in one place a beautiful little cascade fell from quite a height over the rocks. On my right far below lay a narrow valley through which ran a stream, Lycoming Creek, and all along its course lay farms. Beyond the valley were other mountains, dark and wooded. Somewhere near day, I made a raid on a chicken house near the railroad, and captured a fine hen. I did not find a spot sufficiently secluded to camp in until after good day. I had left the railroad and was walking down a lane when I came to a small chestnut tree, which was fairly speckled with ripe nuts. I was up the tree in a minute, and the way the nuts rattled on the ground sounded like twenty drums beating the long roll. I filled all my pockets, the coat pockets so full that nuts dropped on the ground as I walked.

Soon a train came tearing along going South. It was a train of freight cars, loaded with soldiers, many crowded about the broad open doors, just as I had seen in Dixie many a time, except that these soldiers wore blue instead of grey. As soon as they saw me, they set up a yell, never suspecting that I was other than a native Pennsylvanian. I answered back, taking off my hat and waving it, and pointing south, as though to say, "On to Richmond!" adding to myself, "I'll be down there to meet you soon!" It was now about sunrise, Oct. 12th—five days out from Elmira. I was not far from Ralston, which is 54 miles by rail from Elmira. I went off to a rocky hillside, where I made a little fire and roasted Chestnuts, then slept for a time, concealed in the woods.

When dusk came, I took up the march again. Just before dawn I entered a large barn, some distance from a farmhouse, and secured not one but *two* chickens, and so passed thro' Williamsport with two dead chickens under my coat. Near the station were empty trains which had been used to transport soldiers, and lying about on the ground was hardtack, which I gathered up. Then I crossed over the bridge at Williamsport and began to look for a secluded place to camp for the day. It was here that crossing a railroad track, I got a scare. A man approached, evidently intending to speak to me, and I was afraid he was going to ask if I wasn't a rebel prisoner, escaped from Elmira. I was greatly relieved when he inquired if I had found his Naturalization papers, which he had dropped somewhere.

I passed through a field planted with corn, pumpkins, and turnips, all together. Pulling up a turnip or two, I made my way by a little road to the mountain (Bald Eagle) through chestnut woods. Camping here, I made some brief notes, which have aided my memory in recalling details of my escape. My camping place (Oct. 13th) on the side of Bald Eagle was a rough spot, its steep sides being so rocky that it was difficult to find a bare spot large enough to lie down. But I built a fire to keep warm, and slept some.

Late in the afternoon I did my cooking, and went down the mountain, my pockets full of food. Reaching the railroad, I tramped southward, eating broiled chicken and roasted chestnuts as I went. The railroad wound along the west branch of the Susquehanna River. Almost anywhere, a stone thrown to the right would have fallen on a mountain, to the left, in the river. The road here was ballasted with broken rock from the mountain, and as my shoes were worn thin, one sole having a hole in it, I could not step between the ties on the jagged stones. Walking on the cross ties became in time very fatiguing. So I took a little path that led to the river, in the hope of finding there a boat. A few yards brought me to the water, where sure enough there was a boat chained to a stump, but not locked. It was a rowboat with two oars in it. Although experienced in the use of a paddle, I had never had an oar in my hand in my life. At first I handled the oars so awkwardly that the boat turned completely around, as though she intended taking me back to Elmira. But pretty soon I got the hang of the thing well enough to keep her headed in the right direction. I didn't do much rowing but shipped my oars, and lay drifting down, eating chestnuts. I think no "dolce far niente" in Naples Bay was ever sweeter to prince or princess than this idle abandonment to the bosom of the river was to this weary, wandering vagabond. The night was one of unspeakable beauty, and I believe no man in all Pennsylvania enjoyed it as much as I did.

I continued to float down the Susquehanna until the sound of falls or shoals below warned that this mode of travel was no longer safe, and I came ashore. I think I now shoved the boat which had served me so well out into the water. I remember that at this period I had a strange propensity to be as destructive as prudence would allow. I remember heaving a big lump of coal into the canal once, so that no Yankee could use it. A fugitive in enemy country, I had no hesitation about appropriating anything which might aid my escape. I had furthermore the feeling that to destroy anything which might be useful to the enemy was the only way of serving the Confederacy which was open to me at the time. Being by nature thrifty and opposed to all forms of waste, I thus followed a course opposite to my natural instincts.

During the night I passed a lumber yard. By moonlight, I saw lying on a lumber pile a dark object which looked like a coat. A coat it proved to be, a nice clean, business coat, a great contrast to all my other garments. But I put it on under my overcoat, saving the two newspapers I found in the pockets, tearing up a license granted to someone to distill liquor which I also found.

When day came (Oct. 14th) I did not stop as usual, but ventured to travel on by daylight. At Northumberland, 115 miles from Elmira, I got on a freight car loaded with lumber, hiding myself under some of the projecting ends. I had seen that the train was getting ready to start, and soon off we went. At Sunbury, three miles farther on, the train stopped. I lay still, waiting for it to go on. After waiting a long time, I got out to see what was the matter. The engine was gone; evidently the lumber had reached its destination. I went a little way into the town, and seeing a building in process of construction, I went in, thinking I might pick up something useful. I found a plasterer's hat, spotted with mortar. As I thought it suited my general appearance better than the black cavalry hat I had captured in the Wilderness, I put it on, putting the cavalry hat in my bosom for further consideration.

Hearing a train coming, I went back to the station and stood there while passengers got off and on. The engine puffed and started. Saying to myself, "I'll try it on one time," I stepped up on the platform, feeling safer for the concealment of my cavalry hat, the last vestige of the military in my appearance. I stood on the platform, watching through the window for the conductor to come through. Seeing him enter the coach and come slowly down the aisle punching tickets, I waited until he was nearly to the door before stepping down to the bottom step. Hanging on to the railing, my body flattened against the car, I heard a door slam, saw the flash of a lantern. Then I heard another door slam and knew he had passed on to the next car. Swinging back, I sat down on the steps, not venturing to go back inside. And so I rode all the way to Harrisburg, fifty-three miles, arriving at about midnight.

The train did not go on, and I waited for the Baltimore train, determined to try my luck again, for I had fallen in love with this swift and easy mode of travel. When the train for Baltimore was ready, I got on the platform, watched for the conductor as before, and swung outside as he approached. I heard a door slam as he stepped on the platform, and was listening to hear the other door slam, when I felt—a touch on my arm! The car was going too fast to jump. I drew back and faced the conductor, who demanded, "What are you doing out there?"

Since I must tell some story, I gave free rein to my imagination and told a pitiful tale of how I had just got word that my married sister in York was very ill, probably dying, and that being out of work and having no money, I had tried this means of getting to her. The conductor answered gruffly that I ought to be ashamed to try to *steal* a ride—I might have got my brains knocked out against the rocks hanging outside the car that way. Why hadn't I come to him and *asked* instead of trying to *steal* a ride? . . . Now go in the car and sit down, and get off at the very next station, mind you!

I went in and seeing a seat with one old gentleman on it, I took possession of the other half, inadvertently waking the old fellow, who scowled at me, evidently not liking my appearance. I smiled to myself, thinking how his scowl would deepen if he could see the layers of ragged, dirty clothing peeled off one by one, coming at last to a "Johnny Reb" inside them.

The car was so warm, the seat so comfortable, and the aforesaid "Johnny Reb" so weary that soon I was fast asleep. And for all I knew York *was* the next stop, where I had been told to get off, for I heard no other called. I rose, wishing I had placed my sick sister at some point farther on—even in Baltimore—but not daring to overpass the destination I myself had set. What a lift I had had!—84 miles since ten o'clock, and it was now only about two hours past midnight.

I struck out cheerfully, singing "Dixie" as I went. Perhaps good luck had made me over-bold. But actually there was little chance of being over-heard as I tramped down the railroad track at two o'clock in the morning. I kept up the march most of that night and most of next day, crossing Mason's and Dixon's line on foot. There was a post on the side of the railroad marking the line. I felt glad to be even in Maryland.

At daylight Sunday, Oct. 16th I reached Cockeysville, 42

miles from York, 15 miles from Baltimore. Thinking that the roads leading in to Baltimore were probably picketed, I decided that a train, if I could get on one, would probably be safer. As I waited at the station in Cockeysville, a freight train pulled in, loaded with cattle. Federal soldiers armed with rifles were sitting on top of the cars, for the cattle were bound for Grant's army. It would be a cheeky thing to do, but for that very reason it might be my safest course. A Federal train armed with Federal guards was probably the most unlikely means of transportation a fleeing "Johnny Reb" might seek. So with assumed carelessness but a fast beating heart, I climbed the ladder at the end of one of the freight cars and sat down by a soldier!

The soldier made room for me, and began asking questions: Did I live near here? Had I been here when the rebels came? Were there many?

Yes, I lived close by, had been here during the invasion, and the Rebs had swarmed like ants.

Wasn't I "skeart"? And did they do any damage?

I admitted to being pretty badly "skeart," and began pointing out damage they had done—a bridge they had burned, a wheat field they had destroyed.

So friendly we became that I am not sure but the fellow lent me his gun to look at; but as I don't definitely remember having it in my hands, I won't state positively that he did. Anyhow, we examined it together, and if I had wanted to take it in my own hands, I am certain I could have done so without exciting suspicion.

We stopped a good deal on the way, and so made slow time. When we had nearly reached Baltimore, the conductor came around, walking on top of the cars, and asked me where I was going. When I replied that I was going to Baltimore, he said that it was against the company's rules for anybody to ride on the freight trains and that when the train began to slack speed after entering the city, I must jump off. So I did, entering Baltimore at 11 A.M. just as people were going to church.

Though I was gratified to find that very few people seemed to notice me, once in a while a couple would turn around as I passed, and I had a feeling that they wondered if I were a "Johnny Reb." I had to pass policemen, too, with badges on their breasts and cudgels in hand. Putting on a bold front, I walked by in apparent unconcern, though with fast beating heart. I was hunting for North Eutaw Street, and as I avoided asking directions, it was a long time before I found it. Coming at last to the number I sought, the address as I remembered it of Adams' friend, I rang the bell, and the door was opened by a colored maid. But when I asked for Mrs. - - -, the maid said she did not live here. In reply to my further questions, the maid asserted that the lady in question had never lived here, at least in recent years, and that she had never heard the name before.

With a sinking heart, I went down the steps. I had ventured into Baltimore only in the hope of succor—food, clothing, information to guide me in passing through the enemy lines. Through some mistake which was never explained, these would not be forthcoming. Wandering around the streets, trying to decide what to do, I passed a house where, in the basement story, sat a young couple. Through the window I could see them plainly, both blue eyed and fair haired, a newly married couple, I judged. Then I asked for something to eat. He asked her to give me something, and she gave me some bread and mutton. I was sorry to leave that couple, they looked so handsome and so happy, and I felt like unburdening my heart to them. But in this war, all the handsome and happy couples were not on our side; they were pretty evenly divided, I reckoned. If I told them my story as I longed to do, the chances were even that I would betray myself to an enemy.

Again as I walked along, some little boys noticed me and followed at a distance. When I stopped at a corner, one of them came up and offered me an apple, and after a few general remarks, he suddenly looked directly at me saying, "Mister, you look like a rebel." Though I laughed and told the boys that *I* didn't think I looked like a rebel, the remark showed me that I must get out of town right away. If I looked like a "rebel" (so called) to the boys, I must look like a "rebel" to others. I think I was more disappointed at not having found sympathy and friendship in Baltimore than I was in not getting the material help and information that I needed. Just as the sun was setting I passed out of the town, heading westward, for Leesburg where I felt confident of a kind reception from Judge Gray.

Some ten miles beyond Baltimore, I passed through Elicott's Mills in the night, stopping to make raids on apple orchards as I went along. I would enter an orchard, sample several trees, then fill my pockets with those I liked best. It seemed to me that the apples I got that night were even finer than the Pennsylvania apples. They were Winesaps.

Passing a house, I saw some clothes on a line, and I believe it was a pair of trousers I took there. Again I saw a line of them fluttering white in a garden, and I helped myself. At a third stop, I took only stockings, which were all I needed at that time to be fairly well clothed. Before now I had become so disgusted with my filthy state that I had hit upon the expedient of exchanging my dirty ragged garments, one by one, with clean replacements wherever I came upon them on a line. This same night, deciding to investigate a spring-house near the road, and finding it locked, I tried the staple and it pulled right out. I drank one of the large earthen crocks of milk and appropriated a large piece of butter. I laughed to myself to think of the good dame's wonder next morning at finding the emptied crock, the butter gone, and being able to find no place where even a cat could have entered. Having some chestnuts in my pocket, I ate butter and chestnuts as I traveled on.

Once in the night—whether that night or the next I don't clearly remember—I met up with a razor grinder with a wheel on his back, and he told me that he had just come out of a soldiers' camp some 300 yards down the road, where he had been given a fine supper. That was an escape for me! Without this warning, I might have blundered right into a camp of the enemy. As soon as the razor grinder was out of sight, I jumped over the fence on my left and walked thro' the fields. I came to a road which seemed to run southward, perpendicularly to the road I had just left. As I stood debating whether to take this road or keep to the fields for the present, I heard horsemen approaching. Lying in a fence corner, I saw them pass, going towards camp, and in the dim light they appeared to be officers.

Suddenly a dare-devil spirit came over me, and I wanted to look at that Yankee camp. I walked cautiously back along this road to where it joined the road I had just left. Keeping to the bushes alongside, I crept forward until I came to some big rocks. In the woods just beyond, so close I could have tossed a biscuit amongst them, were the soldiers about their fires, cooking, and talking, and walking about amongst the tents. I saw that this was too dangerous. A sudden vision of myself recaptured and hauled back to Elmira made me turn and cautiously retrace my steps. A little way beyond where I had hidden from the officers, I saw a small fire on the side of the road, a picket standing by it with his rifle. I saw that now I must abandon roads and stick to fields and woods, guided by my pocket compass.

It was the night of Oct. 18th that I heard across the fields a faint, continuous sound like that of rushing water, and I made a bee line for the sound. As I drew nearer, it grew louder and louder until there could be no doubt—it was the shoals of the Potomac! I pushed on rapidly and at length, from a hill, I caught sight of the river, and the hills of Virginia beyond. Nothing between me and my country but a ribbon of water, not half a mile wide! I went down toward the river as far as the canal, to reconnoitre. Between the canal and the river was but a narrow strip of land, and there, as I watched concealed, I saw a Federal cavalry patrol ride by along the towpath. I did not move, as I was concealed well enough.

After they passed, I could have swum the canal easily

and reached the river. But I had made other, more grandiose plans for my return to Virginia. I meant to capture a horse and *ride* back. So I went back into a field where I had seen a horse grazing, and caught him without difficulty. Then I produced my string bridle with its wire bit, which I had carried for a long time with this purpose in mind. Slipping it on, I mounted and rode down to the canal. But there my troubles began; the horse refused to enter the water. After trying every method I could think of—spurrings, switchings, getting down and leading—I had to abandon my plan, as daylight came on, and find a place of concealment, as it would not do to try to cross by daylight.

I found a place on the hillside, where some brush had been piled up, and managed to get some wild grapes, which were all I had to eat that day. When night came, I went down to the canal, and crossed over on the gates of the Lock (at Edward's Ferry). On the towpath I picked up a stout, heavy plank apparently used as a sort of gangway to connect with canal boats. Wearing only my shirt and trousers (to avoid being caught in the same plight as after swimming the Rapidan) I wrapped everything else in a tight bundle inside my overcoat, and this I tied securely on the end of the plank, and entered the river. By keeping the rear end of the plank pressed down I kept the front end up and the clothes fairly dry. Stumbling over the rocks in the river, I had nearly reached the Virginia shore, when suddenly I stepped into deep water, and had to swim. I soon landed, exultant, and and the first thing I did was to feel in my pocket to make sure my pocket compass was still there. It was gone! Just before stepping off into deep water, I had checked and found it there. It must have fallen out while I struggled across the current, and would have been borne far away by now. It seemed that Fate had lent it to me to fulfill a mission, and now that I was safe in my own country, had taken it back.

My clothes in the bundle were only a little wet, and I soon had them on, and was on the march to find friends. Traveling along on by-roads and thro' fields, I came at length to a house, and feeling that here I was safe and among friends, I went up and knocked and inquired the way to Judge Gray's. After a while someone called from within, "Who is there?"

"A soldier."

"Union or Confederate?"

"Confederate."

After a little, the door was cracked cautiously, and a survey made of me. When I had explained that I was an escaped Confederate soldier, looking for the home of my friends, the Grays, the man, whose name was Ball, hospitably invited me in, saying that the Grays had moved into Leesburg, and I must stay with them. He conducted me to a little house in the garden, now turned into a school house, where one of his daughters taught some of the neighborhood children, made up a fire, spread a pallet on the floor, and then he showed me how, should I hear cavalry ride up during the night, I must jump out of the back window and run through the corn-field to the woods. Next morning Mr. Ball pressed me to stay with them for several days, resting up, explaining that his own son was a prisoner in a Yankee prison in Washington. So I stayed Thursday with this kind family. Next morning (Friday, Oct. 21st) I went on to Leesburg, seeing none of the enemy or of our men on the way. Being very kindly received by the Grays, I staid with them Friday and Saturday. In Leesburg I met up with a few Confederates, mostly not in uniform. Talking with them, I learned that Mosby was going to start on a raid from a nearby town Monday morning. Though I wished very much to see the famous guerrilla chief, I did not feel myself justified in going a day's march out of my way to gratify this wish.

As I took my leave of my friends the Grays, Sunday morning, Miss Gray presented me with a grey coat, cut in half uniform style, which would pass either as uniform or citizen's dress. This I gratefully accepted. But of the food which she pressed upon me, I would take only a little bread and butter, to lunch on if necessary. Being now in the South,

I had no fear about getting all I needed to eat without robbing hen roosts.

As I walked along the highway, always keeping a good lookout ahead for the enemy's cavalry scouting parties, I came about noon to a man sitting on a fence in front of his house. After answering my questions as to the road ahead, he questioned me about myself. When I had told him the main facts, he cordially invited me to come in and have Sunday dinner, which he said was just ready to be served. I was a little taken aback to find the dining room full of people; but when my eyes lit upon that loaded table, I forgot my embarrassment. Such a table I had not seen for many long months. After a summer of prison fare and then my long tramp, sustained mainly on apples and chestnuts and an occasional stolen chicken, it looked almost miraculous.

I continued on the highway in the afternoon; and as darkness approached, I began looking for a place to spend the night.—not a thicket this time, but a house, for I felt sure these Virginians would take me in. I inquired at several places but everywhere was told that there would be no room for me, as Mosby's men had engaged all their spare room for the night. At length, a little after dark (Sun. Oct. 23/64) I saw a light from a house at some distance from the road, and hoping that Mosby's men had missed this out-of-the-way place, I applied there. But the owner had the same story to tell—Mosby's men had filled him up.

I had been told that Mosby's men had no regular camp like other soldiers. They lived at their own homes, and were advised by couriers to meet at such a time and place when wanted. Thus they could never be overtaken by pursuit. When followed by a greatly superior force, they disbanded, every man seeking his own home or hiding place, and the Federals found no enemy to pursue. Without knowing it, I had stumbled upon their assembly place for tomorrow's raid! And with the result that I could find no shelter for the night, but apparently must camp in the woods, even though back in my own country. As a last hope, I asked if I might sleep in the barn.

The owner said Mosby's men had the barn too. I believed the truth was he feared I might make off with some of the horses. Finally he said he would ask the men whether they were willing that I sleep there that night. Soon he came back and ushered me into a sitting room where two young men sat before a fire. As I entered they looked up, and when I had sat down, they immediately began questioning me. They listened without saying much, except to ask further questions, which obliged me to go back and tell my whole story. When in telling about the Old Capitol, I mentioned Sam Underwood, Ben Crowley, and Woodhouse, they took immediate interest, and soon called in the other men, saying, "Boys, come in here. Here's a man who was with Crowley and Underwood and Woodhouse in the Old Capitol."

Admitting that they had thought I was lying, and had suspected me of being a spy, they now accepted me in the friendliest way, crowding around asking a hundred questions. They invited me to supper, and one of them insisted upon giving up his bed to me, under the pretense that he wanted to sleep in the barn, near his horse. The next thing I saw was a pulling out of pocket books, and a snug little sum was put into my hands, whether or no, with the explanation that I would need it before reaching my destination. It was all done with such soldierly sympathy for the rough time I'd had, that I soon stopped protesting, seeing that I would hurt their feelings by absolute refusal. I felt a great desire to go on this raid with them, and said so. The men said there would be a poor chance, on account of the difficulty of procuring a horse. But they invited me to go to the blacksmith shop, their meeting place, next morning, promising meanwhile to see what could be done.

My new friends reported next morning that it had been impossible to secure a horse. But they introduced me to their chief, who received me kindly, telling me how I had best proceed to avoid the enemy's scouting parties. He advised me to stick close to the mountains.

Mosby's men were nearly all well dressed, in uniforms each

to his own taste, mostly various shades of grey. I noticed that corduroy was much worn, and a handsome uniform it made. Not only were the men better dressed than soldiers ordinarily, but I am quite sure that this band was of better calibre in all respects, physically and mentally, than the general run of soldiers. In the main army, a large proportion of them would have been chosen as officers. Thanking Col. Mosby for his directions and advice, I turned away, feeling really sad as I watched them ride off.

I now made my way along the foot of the mountains, stopping that first night at a house not far from a county-seat called Llangollen, where I asked to be given some supper and a place in the barn to sleep. I was admitted into the house, and ushered to a place by the fire, where were sitting three ladies, all young and pretty, all doing some light work. They listened with a great deal of interest to my story, then conducted me to the dining room with profuse apologies for not being able to furnish me an adequate supper. The house being one of those stately Virginia mansions, and the occupants evidently people of high standing, I could not but construe their apology as expressing regret at not being prepared to set before me a lavish hot meal. What therefore was my astonishment at finding set out on a nice white tablecloth a pitcher of sweet milk and a bowl of chestnuts—and that was all!

They told me that the night before the last one of their negroes had left them and gone to the enemy, taking everything portable. They themselves had just supped on chestnuts and milk, literally the only food they had, and their brother, Lieut. (later Capt.) Bruce Gibson was now at work in the field, pulling fodder by moonlight, having got a few days' leave from the army to save what he could of their crops. Such were the straits the Confederate people were finally reduced to. The Gibsons were of the royal house of Bruce, Scotland, and their place was called Fernue. Though I arose early next morning, I was not early enough to meet Lieut. Gibson, who had already gone to work in the fields.

I traveled that day (Tuesday, Oct. 25/64) for a long distance on an obscure road that ran along the crest of the ridge. I could see far away across the Valley, farms, roads, and villages spread out like a map, through which wound the Shenandoah "like a silver thread." By night I had got nearly as far as Ashby's Gap, where the turnpike runs through from Front Royal to Culpepper C. H. Houses were few and when dark came on, I had found no place to stop. So I kept on walking, finally getting completely lost in the mountains. Selecting a little hollow shut in by rocks, I built a fire and lay down to sleep. Next morning early I got some breakfast at Mrs. Hoffman's in the Gap.

That night (Wednesday 26th) I stopped at a Mr. Craig's, told him my story, and asked permission to sleep in his barn. He was blind, and I could tell at once that he did not know whether or not to believe me. In this neutral ground between Early's and Sheridan's armies were many scouts of both sides, sometimes in their own uniform, sometimes in the enemy's, and it was next to impossible to tell friend from foe. It was in this quarter that I first heard of "Jessie's Scouts," Federal soldiers, sometimes in Confederate uniform, who were always busy between the lines, spying out the movements of our army. The citizens held them in dread. Mr. Craig finally said frankly that he was in doubt, but friend or foe, he would give me supper, and let me sleep in his barn.

It was the next day (Thursday, Oct. 27/64) that I had the supreme satisfaction of being halted by a Confederate cavalry picket, of McCausland's Brigade. Just after dark, I reached Gen. Bradley T. Johnson's headquarters, and reported to him.

General Johnson asked me many questions, the answers to which continually drew out new questions, till finally the General said, "Sergeant, let's start all over. Begin at the beginning and tell us the whole story just as it happened."

"General," I replied, "I'm quite willing. But I tell you— you've got to give me my supper first; I'm desperately hungry."

He laughed and ordered his servant to put out some supper for me on the camp chest that sat in front of his tent and served for a table. Plenty of nice mutton, and I do believe he gave me a cup of coffee! Officers stood or sat around watching me as I ate, not always heedful of the General's request to "Let him alone, boys, till he gets through his supper." But I was hungry and I ate to my satisfaction, and I'm inclined to think that I pretty nearly cleaned out the General's larder.

It was an interesting scene. There I sat across the camp chest, eating heartily, with my eyes so intent upon my victuals that I know I must have looked cross-eyed, while the group of Officers sat and stood around, all watching with amused interest, not altogether heedful of the General's request to "let him alone, boys, till he gets thro' his supper," but every now and then asking some question that I answered as well as a mouthful of hoecake and fresh mutton would let me. Finally I leaned back and said Ugh! They all disposed themselves around to listen, and I began at the beginning and told the whole story. Then began an infinite number of questions again, and it was about midnight before I was let off. The General said at the close, "The Sergeant talks mighty well, don't he?"—a compliment I never had paid me before or since, for I have always borne the reputation of being an indifferent talker.

The question then arose as to where I might be made comfortable for the night, and the General actually went so far as to offer to surrender his own bed to me, which of course I would not accept, saying I was used to sleeping on the ground. So he had blankets brought and I slept just inside his tent, using his saddle for a pillow.

After breakfast next morning, General Johnson gave me a pass to go to Newmarket. In the camp at Newmarket, I met Hoody Hitt from Augusta, who stared at me in disbelief, then asked, "Is this Berry Benson?" From him I learned that for months my family had mourned me as dead, a body found washed up on the beach at Point Lookout the day after my escape having been postively identified as mine by Michael Duffy of Co I, my regt.

In Newmarket I reported to General Early, and from him I got a free pass to Richmond. I went by stage from Newmarket to Staunton, there taking train for Richmond, where I learned that my regiment was now stationed at Petersburg, and was furnished with transportation thither. In Richmond I went to the telegraph office and telegraphed Father: "I am not dead, but alive and well. Just escaped from prison." I later learned that only the last sentence was news, for a few days before, they had learned that the report of my death was false.

Passing by the Spottswood hotel in Petersburg, I saw Capt. Armstrong of Co. K, my regiment, standing on the portico. He knew me at once, and I went with him to camp, thus having no trouble in finding my company. As I passed along, I could hear one say to another, "Sergeant Benson!" Some would have stopped me, but I was too anxious to see Blackwood. Directly I saw him, with his back to me, standing at a fire, cooking. Before I was within ten yards of him, a member of the company saw me and cried out, "Blackwood, here's your brother!"

Blackwood started up, saw me, and made a rush. He pulled my head down and without a word began pounding me heavily on the back with his fist. He pounded so hard that I was obliged to break loose and escape from this odd greeting. The boys crowded around asking innumerable questions. The first thing Blackwood wanted to know was when I had been exchanged. I said I hadn't been exchanged at all— that I had escaped. Then he grabbed me and fell to pounding again.

☆ **8** ☆

Final Resistance

BACK WITH THE SHARPSHOOTERS — DEFENSE OF PETERSBURG —
RETREAT BEGINS — "JUBILO" — APPOMATTOX

☆ ☆ ☆ ☆ ☆ ☆ ☆ ☆ ☆ ☆ ☆

McGowan's Brigade was encamped about 3 miles below
Petersburg, occupying the very point in the line of defense
upon which Grant's heaviest assault would be made, the point
where he would break through on the night of April 1, 1865.
Our picket posts were half a mile or more in front of the
breastworks, being a succession of small earthworks at about
twenty-yard intervals, called rifle pits. Still beyond these,
videttes were posted at night, as close as it was necessary to
the enemy. The breastworks of the enemy in our immediate
front were about a mile and a half away across the fields. And
there they had erected an observatory, on top of which the
signal flag was almost constantly waving. When we had first
passed through Petersburg in April 1861 the city was in its
prime—not the battered, military, woman-deserted city it
now was.

I do believe it was the very next day following my arrival
at camp, after my escape from Elmira Prison, that Gen.
McGowan sent me out on a scout to get some information he
wanted from down about Reams' Station. Not even knowing
where Reams' Station was, I took with me Blackwood and
another Sharpshooter, Crossland, who knew something about
the country. Moving through the woods sometime in the
night, we spied a light. Cautiously approaching, we saw a
low earthwork with four or five men sitting and standing
around a small fire, their arms stacked near the fire.

174

Unable to see them well enough to determine whether they were friends or enemies, we decided that the best thing was to get possession of their arms first, then inquire. So creeping closer, on a signal, we went headlong over the breastwork and had the guns before a man moved. They looked up in greatest astonishment, while we broke into a laugh, for they were the greyest of Johnny Rebs, a cavalry picket so situated that they had little reason to fear a surprise attack. From them we got the information Gen. McGowan wanted.

I was soon given a furlough in honor of my escape from prison. So I started home, being some days on the way, and finally got there. Somewhere, as I was travelling, I heard a soldier on the train talking about Elmira, which at once attracted my attention. I asked had he been there. Yes, he had just been exchanged. He knew about the tunnel, and all, how there was great excitement throughout the prison, and how the tunnel was broken up, being measured and found to be 66 feet long, and our ingenuity was commented upon and admired for making it so crooked (when, forsooth, we had been much astonished at finding we had not gone straight).

Everybody was rejoiced to see me at home, and I enjoyed the change for a few days, but it was only a few days. Sherman was encamped before Savannah, and from Augusta had been sent a Battalion under Maj. George T. Jackson, in which were many of my friends and acquaintances, among them Sergeant John U. Meyer, later mayor of Augusta. In it also were many elderly men excused from military service, and young boys, who did good service, fighting some right tough battles. Soon my fingers began so to itch for my rifle, and my ears to burn so because I idled here at home while the less fit took up arms, that I left home and went to Savannah and staid with the defenders until the evacuation of Savannah was determined upon by the Confederates.

On Jan. 17, 1865 I left home again for Virginia. Making several stops on the way, I arrived at Dunlap's Crossing 2 miles from Petersburg on Jan. 25th, and walked to camp. The reason for stopping the train 2 miles short of Petersburg was that the enemy had advanced their batteries so close to the town that they could easily reach the R. R. with their shells. So to save the locomotives and the cars, and prevent disaster, Dunlap's Crossing was made the terminus.

Blackwood and his friend Norton, a Sharpshooter of Co. A, had built a little cabin, in which the three of us lived for the rest of the winter. Our younger brother, Bradley, who was now sixteen (just the age Blackwood had been when we volunteered), was expected soon to join us. I wrote Father advising that he let Brad come on now, so as to get a little used to army hardships before the summer campaign opened up. About this time Capt. Barnwell said that he could no longer spare two non-commissioned officers from Co. H, and that either Blackwood or I would have to leave the Sharpshooters soon and return to his company. As Blackwood had been a Sharpshooter continuously during the entire existence of the Battalion of Sharpshooters, I knew that the place was his by right, and that if one of us should soon have to leave it, it must be I.

On Monday, March 13 we were told that an attack on the lines was expected. On March 25th it occurred. I shall always remember this fight as of vivid interest, for it took place in the open field in front of us, in ground sufficiently depressed to enable us to look down and see it all. First we saw come marching out from their breastworks a line of the enemy's infantry, winding slowly down along little ravines and gullies until they reached the open ground that stretched for some distance in front of our picket line. There they formed in line, deployed as skirmishers, and advanced to the attack.

Pretty soon our pickets opened fire on them, and they fired in return. As the interval grew less, the sputtering of the rifles grew rapid, until the whole line within rifle reach was taking part in the fight. With a run and a cheer, the enemy closed up and seemed determined to take the works. But the fire of our pickets was too heavy, and after a moment's hesitation, the attackers broke and fled.

But they soon rallied. Still out in the open field where we

could see it all as in a picture, they waited, received reinforcements, and again advanced. Again they were met by a fierce
fire from our pickets, and again they rushed forward with a
shout, in charge, and again they broke in disorder, and fled,
leaving their dead and wounded.

And now a longer time elapsed, and then we saw new
lines of soldiers in blue, filing out from the big breastworks
that ran along the low ridge across the shallow valley, winding
along, half hid by the bushes that skirted the little streamlets,
as they advanced. Soon they formed—not a line of skirmishers
as before, but a solid line of battle. On they came, shoulder
to shoulder, the stars and stripes flying over their heads.
Again the fire broke from one of our rifle pits, extending
to the right and left till the whole line, as far as rifles could
reach, was crackling and sputtering. But forward still swept
the line of blue, heeding neither their dead nor their wounded.
Forward still, with a rush and a shout, the flag well to the
front, and our hearts sink with the fear that they will go over
the works at the first charge. But no, they have stopped! They
stand still and fire, reload and fire. And our men, kneeling in
the pits, take good aim and we can see how busy they are. It
is but a minute before the enemy's line falters, appears about to
break and flee. But look, the color bearer runs forward alone
with his flag. With a shout that rings again, the blue line
follows in a swift charge through our deadliest fire. They
reach the works and turning rapidly to the right and left,
they sweep the line in both directions for a long distance,
taking possession of half a mile of riflepits.

Soon they come to a halt on the left. Our line there has
been strongly reinforced, and they are brought to a stand. A
fresh line of the enemy advances across the field and attacks
in front. They are received so well that they lie down in the
field. We behind the breastworks see this line of blue lying
flat on the open ground, loading and firing; and our men at
the picket line fighting them steadily. And now we get a piece
of artillery in position, and just as we are loaded, a group of
officers on horseback ride up on a little knoll some 8 or 10

hundred yards away, and the piece is aimed at them and fired. The shell strikes in the dust close by, and they ride swiftly away. With artillery to bear up on them, the enemy do not attempt any further advance, but hold what they have, lying securely behind the low mounds that we call rifle pits. Only, they are on the wrong side of them, for they are our pits, thrown up to front the enemy and not ourselves.

Our Battalion of Sharpshooters had been inside the main breastworks when the attack occurred. We were now thrown out front, Co. C going out first, then Co's A and B to connect with it, to sharpshoot. As we became immediately exposed after leaving the breastworks, we had to hide the best we could, by creeping along gullies and depressed ground, taking every advantage of that kind possible. When we were about getting into position, Lieut. Ballinger, lying at my right hand, was struck in the left arm by a bullet which passed on, wounding him also in the leg. He managed to crawl away without rising, which would have drawn many a shot upon him.

The Jones House was a large residence which had stood to the rear of our picket line. But now that the enemy had taken our rifle pits, the house lay between the two advanced lines of foes. It was just getting dusk when we saw some figures moving stealthily about the house. We opened fire, but were unable to drive them away. Presently a bright flame shot up, then another. In a few minutes the house was one huge flame of fire, lighting up the fields for a great distance around.

When night came and the fighting was stopped, the Sharpshooters moved to the right and connected with a line of pickets sent out from the Brigade, and we threw up a new line of pits. Early Sunday morning, March 26th, sharpshooting from these new pits began. With several others, I managed to get into an old pit that lay, perhaps as much as 80 yards in advance of our present line, where we got several very fair shots. We kept our position till about dark. Indeed, after being discovered there, it was too dangerous to attempt to

leave it. As the slightest exposure of a man was certain to
call forth a number of shots, some of the boys concluded to
try the time-honored dodge of holding up a dummy. So
they tied a coat to a stick or a ramrod, and placing a hat on it,
poked it up cautiously. Pop, went the rifles! Dummy was
dropped, and a shout went up from the enemy. One more
"rebel" killed! After a little Mr. Dummy looked up again,
and again the rifles blazed away. The trick was played for
some time before they found it out. And even then we could
sometimes fool them by moving the dummy along as though it
were a man walking.

Before dawn Monday, March 27th we united with other
Sharpshooters of the Division and passed out of our breastworks in front. We did not know where we were going until
we were halted and formed in line-of-battle, close to our
own picket line. But on finding ourselves joined by other
Sharpshooters we had guessed something of the purport. About
400 men, picked out of the whole Division, all Sharpshooters,
we were bound upon an adventure in which each Brigade's
Battalion determined to outdo every other Battalion in the
affair that was to come off.

The officers passed along the line the instructions received
from the commander of the expedition. We were to advance
cautiously and silently across the field upon the enemy's picket
line, speaking no word and firing no shot until discovered by
the enemy. It was the enemy himself who was to sound our
charge by his first challenge or shot. As we drew nearer the
enemy, the snapping of sticks, the rustlings of brush seemed
to me so loud that I could not understand how we went so
far undiscovered. We could see the low mounds looming ahead
of us in the gloom, when silence was broken by the first cry
of "Halt!" and the ring of a rifle.

In the same instant a wild Confederate yell split the air.
A solid rush, and we leaped over the works amongst the half
awakened foe, who barely fired a score of shots as they fled
in confusion. To the right and left we swept, clearing the
line as we went. A few scattering shots, and our surprise and

victory were complete. All that day we held the line and kept up sharpshooting. At night we retired to an interior line which had been constructed during the day. We were then relieved and marched back to camp.

On the night of March 29th we moved down the works to the right, the Sharpshooters thrown in front as skirmishers, and marched to Burgess's mill. It was an ugly night, dark and threatening, with some rain. The roads were soon trodden into slush, and we stumbled along, our feet heavy with the mud that clung to them. Moving by the right flank, we had left our winter quarters never to return, but we did not know it then. Though there were fearful and doubting hearts among us to whom the power of the enemy was so plain that they feared we would soon be a conquered people, there was no prophet among us to tell that we were even then writing the last few pages of our war history.

By the right flank we plodded through mud and darkness to Burgess's Mill where the Plank Road crosses Hatcher's Run, and there we halted, at an angle in the works, where they turned square to the right, to protect the right flank of the army as it lay in position round Petersburg. As we stood there in the early dawn, General McGowan, riding by, called me to him. He asked how I would like to be an independent scout, with a few men under me. I replied that of all things, it was what I most desired. He then said that General Lee had told him that he intended giving me such a position, and that it would be done as soon as the present movement had quieted down, and he could give his attention to it.

I felt very much elated, and set about picking out in my own mind whom I would take as companions, and continued debating this question while we moved further to the right and took position in a wood. In front of us, the trees had all been felled for a width of about 400 yards, the tops lying toward the front, to impede the advance of an enemy. The Sharpshooters were then thrown out in front and took position as pickets along a line of rifle pits on the farther side of the cleared space.

Co. A was on the right of the Battalion as usual. When we got into position, we found we were not supported on our right, there being no other pickets to connect with. It was the duty of the Lieutenant commanding the company to send out good men and endeavor to *find* our support. But as Lieut. Hasell was on furlo', I looked around for his replacement. The men were laughing, making game of someone, and when I asked, they pointed out to me our Lieutenant skulking behind a big pine tree, the only tree of any size along the line—skulking, too, when the fire was not very warm.

Being the ranking Sergeant present, and no commissioned officer, I instructed my brother Sergeants to say to the men that I was in command. Then taking several men, I moved quickly to the right, posting the men just close enough together to see one another. Then I went on alone, and guided by the sound of firing, I found our neighboring pickets. There was an interval of several hundred yards between their left and our right, but by stretching our lines both ways we managed to keep in communication, except for a bare open space of about 60 yards, very much exposed, with no rifle pit or other protection for a Sharpshooter. We were skirmishing pretty much all day, but at long range, and I don't think anybody on our side was hurt. What became of our lieutenant I don't know, but I reported the case to Capt. Dunlop, commanding the Battalion. I never saw the Lieutenant afterward but once. That was in the confusion of the Retreat, when I saw him marching along by himself.

There had been no danger in leaving the gap of about 60 yards during the daytime, the position being so exposed that enemy penetration was impossible. But when twilight came on, I posted a line of men there. I had hardly moved when I was called back; they had already got a prisoner. He was a large young man of about 25, a Sergt. Major, who said he was from Wisconsin, pronouncing his "Ss" with a sharp sort of lisp. I took him for a keen fellow, and when the two men I detailed to conduct him to Capt. Dunlop had started off as nonchalantly as possible with their guns over their shoulders,

I remembered how I had knocked the gun off a guard's shoulder when I myself was a prisoner. So I stationed two men behind him with instructions to shoot him upon the least attempt at escape, making sure that he heard these instructions issued.

About 9 o'clock that night we heard a cowbell out in the field, near the enemy's line. It kept shifting about, gradually getting nearer, and many thought it didn't ring naturally. The suspicion arose that a party of the enemy were ringing the bell, endeavoring to entice one or two Confederates to come out in the hope of getting fresh beef. To find out, I went out in front, through the old field, and pretty soon the bell began to move toward me, slow at first, then faster, and presently here came, passing swiftly along, a shadowy body, which I could barely distinguish in the dim light. Taking the best aim I could, I fired, and then away it went, a genuine cow-gallop, but whether I hit my mark I could not tell. The last we heard of the bell was away off in the distance. If anybody ate beef that night, it must have been the blue-coats.

Next day, March 31st, we remained on the picket line— I believe without rations. Some time during the day, the skirmishing on our right, which had been going on all day, suddenly waxed hotter. Soon we saw in the woods beyond the field, the moving figures of the enemy giving way before our men advancing. It was our Brigade advancing in line-of-battle, driving the enemy before it. It was a beautiful sight. As the battle grew closer and louder, we could see the enemy retreating through the woods, stopping behind trees to fire, then hurrying off again, our men following close. A flank fire from our pits galled the enemy as they retreated. Past us the two lines went, about 400 yards obliquely across our front, till foe and friend disappeared in the forest, and the sound of musketry grew fainter and fainter.

But soon there was a fresh roar; evidently the pursuit had been checked by reinforcements to the enemy. Steady it seemed to be for some time, then the sounds grew louder— our men were in retreat! We stood up behind our rifle pits to see. Again the two lines passed across our front, this time in reverse order. We gave the much augmented enemy force volley after volley from our line of rifle pits, till they were beyond reach.

When they had driven our men fairly under cover of their breastworks, the enemy drew up at the edge of the open field in our front, with the evident intention of punishing us for the part we had taken in the battle. In solid double line of battle they formed, and out from the woods into the field they marched, flags flying. We at once opened on them from our whole line, and a long line of Sharpshooters it was, whose fire they had to stand. Our fire was a converging one, and we did good execution.

Our fire was so hot that before the enemy had advanced far, they stopped suddenly and lay down—all except a few officers whom we could see standing up, endeavoring to urge their troops forward. We could see them waving their swords over their heads, the blades flashing in the sunshine. I think there were three flags crowded together, right in the center of the group. The color bearers were lying down holding their flags upright. And how we did keep pouring the bullets into them, the flags for a mark!

Presently, down fell a flag, the color bearer shot as he lay on the ground. Then up it rose again; down again; up again! The flags continued to tumble and rise, while the men lay still on the ground, the swords of the officers whirling and flashing as they tried to bring their men to a charge. I had a Spencer rifle, given me by my brother, who had captured it in some battle. It shot seven times without reloading and I had only 40 cartridges. I stood on a stump where I had a clear, open view, and fired so fast that once I had to stop to let my gun cool. A man in the pit beside me was wounded, shot in the head.

At last the enemy rose, and raising a shout, rushed forward, their three flags streaming, headed straight across the field to where Co. A. held the line. We staid till they were close up, delivering our fire at short range. Then we fled from the works across the tangle of felled trees, back to the main breastworks, where our line-of-battle stood. Close behind followed the blue-coats, and such a volley of bullets as they poured in amongst the felled trees and bushes through which we were with difficulty clambering. But they were stopped by this obstacle and did not pursue to the main breastwork.

After a while we moved out front again to reconnoitre, and advanced unmolested clear back to our rifle pits, and found the enemy had gone. My knapsack which I had left in the hurry of retreat, had been rifled, and everything in it that I cared for, taken. My blanket lay on the ground though, and that was all I had any business lugging round. It was a dear fight for them; their losses had been heavy, while ours had been astonishingly light. In the battle in which our Brigade had fought that day, the Colonel of our regiment was killed—the *only* man killed in the regiment. Col. McCreary was from Barnwell District, and had entered the Regiment as Captain of Co. A from Barnwell.

Being kept on the picket line that night without relief, I was roused from a nap about 2 o'clock by a messenger from Gen. McGowan, ordering me to report to him at once. As our Brigade had moved further down the breastworks to the right, I had to go about two miles to reach the General. He wanted me to go out scouting in front to find the enemy's position, numbers, movements etc. He drew for me by the campfire a sketch of the position of our lines, which I still have. I was to go out till I reached the White Oak Road, near the Dabney house, and in that neighborhood he thought I would find the enemy. I took with me Shade Thomas (of 12th Regt., I think—not a Sharpshooter) and at daylight we left our men lying on their arms, and advanced through the uncertain woods.

At length we reached the White Oak Road, the Dabney House on our left. Presently we heard rifle shots in that direction, and then horses' feet galloping. And here came a Confederate cavalryman down the road, his horse bleeding from a wound just received. He told us that the enemy had attacked our cavalry picket post near the Dabney House. We hurried through the woods, to take part in the fight. But when we came in sight, nobody was there. Our picket must have been taken, for not far away we saw a long line of Federal infantry on the march. We could have sent half a dozen bullets amongst them—at least Thomas could, but I hadn't a single cartridge, having shot my last Spencer cartridge the day before, and been unable to get others. But we had been sent out to scout, not to sharpshoot. So after watching them some time, we went back and reported.

Later in the day we were sent out again to the White Oak Road, this time to the left of the Dabney House. There we came in sight of the enemy's breastworks in an open field, and we saw some of their men about the house. Reporting this, I was ordered to proceed with two or three men as scouts, while at a distance behind us should follow the Sharpshooters, and behind them the Brigade in line-of-battle. I took Ben Powell and Shade Thomas, and posting one to the right of me, one to the left at a distance of between 50 and 100 yards, we moved forward through the forest until we came to its edge, which ran along the White Oak Road. Beyond, in the open field lay the breastworks of the enemy. Though we could see no sign of anybody about them, there was no way of knowing that they were not hidden behind them waiting for us to come up. So it was with fast beating hearts that we walked right up to the breastworks and mounting them looked over. What a sight met our eyes! Not a man anywhere, but knapsacks, guns and provisions of all kinds, including dead cattle, half skinned, some of it cut in pieces for cooking. We signaled to the Brigade which stood waiting in the edge of the woods. They advanced, and the breastworks were in possession of our soldiers.

But where was the enemy? Again the Scouts were ordered to advance and the Sharpshooters to follow. On through the open field we went again. My feet had begun to pain me, because the soles of my shoes were worn through, and I stopped long enough to exchange them for a pair of boots

that I saw lying, but the boots were not much better. Beyond
this broad field was a large wood of small pines. Directly in
my front the field projected into the woods, forming a sort of
"bay," so that both Powell and Thomas, on my right and left,
had already entered the woods whilst I was still in open field,
the woods partly encircling me at a distance of about 40 feet.
Turning my eyes to the right, I was astounded to see at the
edge of the woods three of the enemy, who began beckoning me with their hands to "come in." What a fix I was in!
With an unloaded gun and without a cartridge to load it, my
first impulse was to obey. But the thought of Elmira Prison
flashed into my mind, and with it the actual *feeling* of being
in prison. And this feeling prompted my next, reckless move—
to play a bluff game and capture *them*. Throwing my gun
in the position of ready, I called out, "Surrender! You are
cut off and surrounded. Surrender!"

They did not stir, but I saw that I had alarmed them.
They evidently thought that they *might* be cut off from their
line in the rear, and they stood irresolute. This hesitation
assured me of victory. I cried out, "Throw down your guns
and surrender, or I will shoot you!" and I threw my gun
to my shoulder. Down went two of their rifles and two came
running toward me, the other still hesitating.

I cried again, "If you don't throw down that gun, I'll
shoot!" and I took aim. Down went his gun, and he came also.
With a heart overflowing with joy at my fortunate escape,
I put my prisoners in front of me and marched them to the
rear, till I landed them safely with the Sharpshooters.

One of our boys pointed out one of the prisoners, saying,
"Sergeant, that fellow's got on a mighty good pair of boots!"

"Well, let him keep them," I said. Then I looked at
the old ill fitting boots which were already paining me, and
decided that it was my duty to keep myself fit for service.
So I told my captive to sit down and we would swap boots.
I had never before this taken *anything* from a prisoner.

Powell and Thomas, finding themselves without a leader,
had come back. But now, having got rid of my prisoners,

we advanced again and pushed through the pine woods until we came to a field beyond. There we saw the enemy's works well manned. Going back, we reported to the General, and the Brigade was marched back to our own works.

At night (Apl. 1) the Sharpshooters, much fatigued from continuous picket duty and loss of sleep, were permitted to remain at the breastworks to get a night's sleep, while men of the line were put in front as pickets. But it had hardly grown dark, when the pickets began firing. The enemy were advancing through the tangle of felled trees and bushes. Our pickets became so hard pressed that they had to give way and fall back behind the breastworks. Our works were thinly manned, and we had to keep shifting from one point to another, where the advance of the enemy seemed to threaten most. At one point they came so close that we made some of them come over the breastworks and surrender. These were Germans and could speak no English.

The breaking of twigs and the tramping of the enemy went on for a long time, we keeping up a steady fire, aiming at the noise. Once our firing was briefly suspended whilst I went over the breastwork out in front. But in the dark I could learn nothing more than that they were slowly drawing near our works, apparently with the intention of making a charge. But they kept shifting about, harassing us at one point then another, keeping us shifting to meet one threat, then another. Our fire must have been a hot one for them, although we could not see them or know what execution we were doing.

At last, to our great relief we heard a loud voice call out in command: "Skirmishers—in retreat—March!" And then we heard them going back through the bushes until they were out of ear-shot.

And now the Sergeant Major of our regiment, Wm. Delph, an old school mate, came in from the front, where he had been all the time amongst the enemy. Having been on picket duty, he had been trapped in the sudden attack. Wearing a blue overcoat, he had been mistaken by the enemy in the dim light for one of their own men, even talking with them. He said our fire was a terrible one; to escape it, he had lain down behind one of the felled trees. Waiting there until after the enemy retreated, he had escaped capture.

The next day, Sunday, April 2, 1865, the Sharpshooters were put out in front again, to picket. While we were on the picket line, orders were brought to us to retreat back to the works and follow the army. The retreat from Richmond had begun!

We learned that at half past three that morning (April 2nd) the enemy, five miles on our left, had stormed and carried the defenses of Petersburg, entering the works at the very point held by our Brigade all through the winter. At 7 o'clock Fort Gregg had been taken. That fort was in rear of our line of breastworks. Our Corps Commander, Lieut.-Gen. A. P. Hill, had been killed, Petersburg and Richmond evacuated, and the whole army was in retreat.

Reaching the breastworks, the Sharpshooters pushed on to overtake the Brigade, I remaining with a handful of picked men to break up numbers of rifles, to prevent their falling into enemy hands. Taking a gun by the stock we swung the barrel violently against a tree, which bent it out of all shape, and so rendered them useless. Then I sent a man down each street, to see if any skulker waited concealed, intending to be captured by the enemy. Sure enough, seated before a fire cooking a corncake in one of the cabins was a Confederate soldier—or rather a being who had passed as a soldier. A huge pile of miscellaneous plunder which he had gathered on the bunks told the tale without words.

When I ordered him out, he began to grumble, and two of the Sharpshooters jerked him out. Being sent back in for his cartridge box and gun, he came out heavily loaded with loot, most of which I ordered him to throw down. Ordered to march, he moved off so slowly that I threatened to shoot him unless he moved faster. Then he began to whine. Finally, seeing that he would be a continual impediment, I told Blackwood (who was sadly in need of shoes) to take a new pair of boots he had swinging over his shoulder and let him go. He protested and blubbered so at having to give up this extra pair of shoes to a comrade whose feet were practically on the ground, that the boys itched to shoot him for the deserter which he undoubtedly was. I never have been certain that I was right in making them let him go.

When I told the boys that we were to linger as a rear guard, they were willing enough. Pretty soon we saw the enemy coming in pursuit, and we began sharpshooting. Making a stand at any favorable point, we fought their advance skirmishers until they would begin to flank us, and then we would hastily retreat, to take up a fresh stand. Once we crossed a large creek over a bridge, which we intended burning behind us. But before we could set fire to it, some of the enemy already on that side came running through the woods, and we had to move quickly, leaving it unburnt.

About noon we overtook the three Brigades, which had halted in a field near the South Side Railroad, and there had thrown up a low embankment, to give their pursuers a fight. Besides McGowan's, I think they were McRae's and Archer's Brigades. We let the enemy advance till within good reach, and then opened on them heavily, and the Battle of Sutherland's Station began. The enemy came up in pretty good order, confident of going over; but they soon faltered under our fire, then broke and fled to the woods, some of us jumping out of the breastworks and pursuing until they gained cover. Again they formed and advanced, and again we drove them back as before.

And now a long time ensued, the enemy making no advance except to throw Sharpshooters well forward, who kept up a steady fire. There was a road about 400 yards in front of us, running nearly parallel with our lines, where their Sharpshooters found some good protection. I had reluctantly thrown away my Spencer, for which I could find no ammunition, and taken up an Enfield. I remember setting the sights of my Enfield for a distance of 400 yards. We had some right lively sharpshooting, during which I saw something I had never seen before during all the fights I had been in. I had loaded my rifle and raised up to fire, when in the air right out in front I saw a little black spot. Instantly the thought flashed through my mind, "That's a bullet!" Before I could move a muscle, whiz it went, close to my left ear. I had often in battle seen shells and pieces of shells on the wing, but never before a bullet.

Within six paces of where we were was a piece of field artillery, with four horses; and the artillerists, to protect themselves from the enemy's sharpshooters, lay down behind the earthwork, amongst us. But the standing horses, being plain to see, were a fair mark, and it was but a little while before one of them was struck down, then another, and presently another, and then the last. I shall never forget the piteous looks of one of them, wounded, as he lay on his side in his harness every now and then raising his head to look back at his wound, then laying his head on the ground again, without a sigh or a groan; it was indeed piteous.

After a while, firing was heard on our left, which grew heavier as it approached nearer. It became evident that our line was being flanked on the left. And now the enemy advanced again on our front. We engaged them, but had fired only a few rounds when we saw our men on the left fleeing. The break kept coming down the line till it reached us. Only Blackwood, Henson and I of the Sharpshooters waited as a rear guard till the enemy reached the breastworks, when we fired our last shots. A shower of bullets whizzed past us as we now ran.

In the middle of a large cornfield we overtook the three Brigades, heading now for the Appomattox River, with the intention of crossing to its *north* side to escape our pursuers, and join the army from Richmond. We reached the river in the late afternoon, finding one small boat which would carry perhaps four men, as our only means of crossing. There followed a sort of panic, the men asking questions which no one could answer. The Generals met in consultation and it was decided to push as rapidly as possible up the river until we reached some crossing—where or what it would be not even the Generals knew. It would not be a *ford*, however, for the river was swollen high with rain.

All this time the boat had been plying backward and forward, carrying as many as it could. A few men chose to remain behind, hoping to avail themselves of this means of escape. The rest of us (Probably not more than 1000 to 1200 men) turned our faces up the stream and in Indian file followed a footpath along its banks, hoping every minute to reach some bridge or ferry. In single file the Brigades stretched out, reaching far up and down the river. At length (about full dark) there was a halt, and the troops were collected in a little hollow. We all lay down on the wet leaves in the wood, tired and hungry, and awaited orders.

Hundreds of questions were asked and doubts freely raised of our ever getting out of this scrape. Here we were, 3 Brigades, cut off from the rest of the army, a swollen river in front, and Grant's army pressing on behind! It was all too true and too plain, and it became as plain as possibly could be that if the enemy did come, even in very small force, our men were so badly demoralized that they would make no fight. Officers were as ignorant and helpless as the men.

After trying in vain to learn something of our plans and prospects, I went to Gen. McGowan, whom I found lying down with some officers among the leaves. He frankly told me that none of the general officers even knew where to find a crossing, and that they had just sent out to see if some house could be found where information could be got.

Seeing capture staring us all in the face, I determined not to be taken prisoner again if I could help it. Going back to the men, I called on the Sharpshooters—all who wished—to follow me, that I was going to find Lee's army. A good many came, not only from the Sharpshooters, but others. I talked to them a little, telling them it was plain to me that to stay long in this place would be to make prisoners of all of us, and that I meant to escape. "But," I said, "the probability is that we shall march all night, and march *hard*. It is mighty little rest I shall give you. My aim is to keep up the river until we come to some crossing. If we find none, our march must have been long enough, at daylight, to have carried us beyond reach of the enemy."

Then some of the men who knew what I meant by hard marching and dreaded it, dropped out. I started off with 15 men besides myself, one of them, a young fellow, barefoot. And a hard march we made. Coming to a creek flowing into the Appomattox, and too wide and deep at its mouth to cross, we marched up its banks until we came to a floating bridge of rails, probably thrown in the day before by retreating troops. Lodged against the trees, the rails made a passable bridge, though an unsteady one. We crossed without mishap and took up our march again, heading for the river. We had not gone far before we heard firing, and were told by some soldiers we met that it was our cavalry fighting the enemy's cavalry.

Going on, we came to three Federal soldiers sitting calmly by the roadside, who, on being questioned, said they were prisoners. Their guards in the hurry of the retreat had gone off and left them! Thinking that it would never do to leave three prisoners there to await the arrival of their own men, I made them get up and march. At the next halt, my barefoot man came to me and said: "Sergeant, I'm barefoot. Won't you let me take the shoes of one of them?" I hesitated but decided that if it came to a choice of who must get knocked up, better let it be the Federal than the Confederate. So I said, "Yes, take the shoes but nothing else." Some of my men seemed disposed to make a thorough overhauling of the prisoners, but I would allow nothing to be taken but the shoes. Later their Sergeant-Major expressed his thanks to me and asked me to accept from him in token a silver piece, which he said was a florin. I declined it, saying he would need it in prison. Privately I knew our chance of prison was a precious lot bigger than his! Before dawn we reached a small camp of our soldiers—I think they were Texans—and turned our prisoners over to them. Some of the men were already complaining of being tired out, Blackwood as much as any, and I had to allow more frequent rests. When we were about a mile and a half from a point on the river where we had been told there was a ferry, Blackwood declared he could go no further. As we had been told that the ferry had been dropped down the river till morning, to conceal it from the enemy, I made a halt, and we all lay down in the woods near the road to get a little rest and sleep.

At daybreak, Monday April 3rd we resumed the march, soon reaching the ferry, where we were in the second boatload to be taken across that morning. After crossing a large wet field we learned from some soldiers that our Brigade was organizing at Goode's Bridge on the Appomattox, and we headed for it. Later in the day, we being entirely out of rations, I detailed Blackwood and another Sharpshooter to go to a farmhouse and see if anything could be had to eat. They returned promptly with a quantity of meal. Gen. Heth, who now commanded Hill's Corps, Gen. Hill being killed, happened to be at the farmhouse. In answer to his questions, the boys had told him of our little band of sixteen keeping together, and of our hard march, and General Heth had instructed the owner of the house to let them have 16 rations of meal, charging it to the Confederacy.

But we had no meat, and I detailed Blackwood again as a forager to secure some, by impressment if not otherwise obtainable. He went off with a companion, and before long a rifle shot announced that they had come upon game. Shortly after, they hove in sight, each with a pig! I scolded them for killing more than one, but Blackwood said it was an accident— he had shot at one and killed two! It was nearly night when this took place, and at dusk we halted in a pine wood, built a rousing fire, and while some busied themselves about getting wood and water, others went to try to borrow something to cook in. They soon came back with a big washpot. The pigs were skinned and cleaned, the pot put on, both pigs in it, and most of us wrapped up in our blankets to snatch an hour's sleep, while two agreed to take turns in watching the pot. I left orders with the cooks to wake me as soon as the pigs were done, that we might resume our march, lest the enemy, pushing on from Richmond, make us prisoners.

But it was late in the night when I was waked, and the pigs boiled almost to a jelly. I recognized the sound of troops marching along the road close by, and was told by the cooks that it was Longstreet's men, retreating from Richmond. One had been out to the road and found out. After eating, we again took up the march, making our way amongst Longstreet's men as best we could. We made another stop late in the night, resting till daylight.

Next morning, April 4th, we started early. Being now pretty well rested, we made as good time as possible amongst the straggling troops that now thronged the road. I do not remember seeing anywhere an organized body. Each man seemed to be for himself, getting along as fast or as slow as he was able. Amidst this helter-skelter, dejected crowd, we marched in order, with arms at the "right shoulder." As we passed the weary, exhausted groups, they stared in amazement to see our little band of sixteen, still preserving discipline and still better, cheerfulness. And it was more than one compliment that we received from the old, ragged, weather-beaten, war-worn soldiers that had followed Longstreet in many a battle to victory, as they now followed him in defeat. And a compliment from such tongues was indeed a compliment, sweeter today to remember than would be the most glowing praise from smoother tongues.

Totally unable to take in the fact that this was indeed defeat, regarding it as a temporary set-back which must be overcome, we marched in order, as neatly as on drill, keeping step to the song that Reuben Ruff sang in a clear, ringing voice, one of the best voices in our camp. The song was "Jubilo," a negro song first sung by the Yankees, later becoming a favorite amongst Confederates. Like schoolboys on a holiday, we joined in Ruff's chorus at the top of our lungs so that woods and hills along our march fairly rang with shouts of "Jubilo." Even the exhausted veterans plodding wearily on seemed to catch the infection and become more cheerful. Glad to be out of the cramped and tiresome breastworks, feeling now not so much depressed with recent defeats and evidences of the enemy superiority as happy to be again in woods and fields, we were full of hope that again we might trap and ambush and lie in wait. Maybe in a few days the enemy might find us assailing him unaware, falling upon him flank and rear as we were used to do when Jackson led us.

At Goode's Bridge we found the remnants of our Battalion—between 200 and 300 men, and the story they had to tell proved the wisdom of our undertaking. They had been surprised on the bank of the river by the enemy's cavalry, and without making a fight, it had been every man for himself. Numbers of the men jumped into the river and swam across. The colors were hastily stripped from the staff and buried, and in a few minutes everything was over, those who had escaped fleeing as fast as feet would take them, the others falling prisoner to the enemy.

Of our whole battalion of Sharpshooters—three companies—only forty were left, of which we made 16. Lieut. Hasell, in command of Co. A, had been home on furlough; he returned to us at this point of our retreat.

From Goode's Bridge on, our march was one of unremitting fatigue, hunger, trouble, and disaster. I do not remember that we had rations issued at any time, but must shift for ourselves as best we could. The march was kept up day and night. We rested at odd and uncertain intervals, sleeping as we lay down with gun in hand, bundled up with whatever baggage we carried, which was rarely more than blanket, haversack, canteen, and cartridge box. As we marched along in column, many short halts occurred, caused by some obstacle in front. At first I would stand waiting, as did nearly all, expecting every moment to go on. But soon, along with many others, I fell into the practice of lying down whenever there was a halt, and so got many a good little rest, for in our exhausted state it took but a moment to drop off to sleep.

Harassed on all sides by the enemy's cavalry, we of the

Sharpshooters were often thrown out on the flank, and had more or less skirmishing to do. Every hour brought news of the capture or burning of portions of our wagon trains, while wagons, broken down horses, pieces of artillery, stragglers, and all kinds of munitions of war were being abandoned to fall into the hands of our pursuers. A fusillade off at a distance would tell of a descent upon a wagon train by their cavalry. Then a column of smoke rising above the tree tops would tell of its capture and destruction.

Not much of what was captured, however, was of service to the enemy, for we were too poor to own food, clothing, blankets, or anything but powder and lead—and not enough of that. The horses were mere skeletons, and fell all along the road, dying out of sheer exhaustion and starvation, and the men were in not much better condition. Straggling became the rule rather than the exception. From sheer weakness and lack of sustenance, many a brave man lagged then behind his command who had never lagged before. The 8,000 who drew up that morning before Appomattox were not 8,000 bodies; it was 8,000 *souls* which still dragged along with them their unwilling bodies, whether or no.

There are many incidents of this march which have passed entirely out of my memory, whilst others stand out as fresh and distinct as if they happened thirteen days ago instead of now thirteen years. But in the general confusion of the times, I no longer remember their order. I don't remember when or where it was that we formed line-of-battle under artillery fire from the enemy and prepared for battle. But I remember watching a Georgia Colonel struggling valiantly to straighten out his men. Finally he posted himself under a persimmon tree and called out: "Dress on this 'simmon tree, men; dress on this 'simmon tree." Even amidst all the tragic circumstances the scene struck me as very funny.

I remember that at Farmville the rumor circulated that at last we should draw rations, and we saw men come on with some rice and meat; but the little they had was distributed in such a catch-as-catch-can manner that very few got anything, and we began to disperse in search of much needed food. But we were at once recalled to march to the relief of our cavalry. We had got out of town and were ascending a hill when we were halted and counter-marched, the idea being to put the bridge between us and the enemy as quickly as possible. A dense column of our soldiers was already passing over the bridge when we reached it, but we had got to the other side when the report of a cannon rang out, and a shell burst before us in the road, so close were the enemy upon us! Another shot and another! To escape the shells, we scattered through the fields, offering no especial strong mark to the gunners.

As I ran up a low hill, the shells bursting all around, I came upon a camp fire abandoned by its maker, and upon it sat boiling a pot full of peas. The fear of getting killed was strong, I admit, but hunger was a match for it. I saw Lieut. Hasell running by and called to him to come quick. Running the barrel of my gun through the handle of the pot, I gave him the butt, took the muzzle myself, and off we went amidst the crackling of the shells, bearing to a place of safety our pot of peas. But alas for human endeavor! When we finally reached a place where we could stop, we found the peas but half done, so turned the pot over to Owens to cook while we went on to the picket line with the Sharpshooters. When I next saw the pot (which was the next day, I believe) there was not a pea left to tell the tale. Fortunately while out scouting, I stumbled upon a haversack which somebody had dropped and found something to eat in it; at Farmville I had got nothing.

The evening of the 7th—or it may have been the 6th—we were halted and the Sharpshooters thrown out to the left. Advancing to post ourselves along a low hill, we saw the enemy establishing their skirmish line in an open field, carrying it right through a large farmhouse. I proposed to Lt. Hasell that we take half a dozen men, sneak up close to the house, storm it, and take prisoner the seven or eight men posted there. He consented, and with Blackwood and some two or three others we made our way without discovery along a wooded ravine to within 200 yards of the house. Then getting down on hands and knees, taking advantage of bushes and clumps of grass, and at last getting flat down on our bellies, we crawled so close to the house that it would have been but a short, quick run to reach it. But after carefully looking over the ground, Lieut. Hasell came to the conclusion that it might cost us more than the game was worth. For if we should lose one or two men in the charge, we would be ill paid by the capture of a few prisoners, though he did not doubt that we could take the house if we made the venture. So, without firing a shot, we crawled back undiscovered, and took place again on our skirmish line.

This must have been on the 6th, for I have it clearly in my memory that it was the following day, the 7th, that we were skirmishing with the enemy in an oak wood, the Sharpshooters well concealed by the trees. I was behind a large oak tree, only now and then getting a shot, which was always answered by half a dozen of the enemy, who were also well concealed at a little distance among the oaks. Immediately in my front was a thin wood of low pine bushes or saplings, too open, I thought, for the enemy to occupy. After a while I saw a puff of white smoke shoot out among these pines. Then came another puff, and a bullet sang by my head. Watching closely, I finally saw the dark figure of a man as he shifted his position a little, so that for the moment he stood exposed from the waist upward above a pine bush. The distance was about 150 yards.

I leveled my rifle and fired, and when the smoke cleared away he had disappeared, whether struck or not I could not tell. But the interest of this shot—an abiding one to me— is that *it was my last shot of the war.*

Two days more, and that long series of days of toil and exposure, hunger, cold, fatigue, and danger—days that seemed then as though they would never draw to an end—were over; and the warm sunshine in which we basked as we lay on winter noons by the side of our log-cabins; the white moonshine of the nights that gleamed upon our rifle-barrels as we stood on our picket posts; the ring of rifle and axe; the tramp and rustle of thousands on the march—all these were to be no longer facts, and present consciousness, todays and tonights. They were to become far-away yesterdays, were to fade out and backward into mere dim history. And while I write it seems as though now, in being obliged to say "It *was*," some great bundle of treasure-holding years have been torn out of my life, some sweet thing slipped out of my grasp, and like a silver coin dropped into deep water. I see it slipping away, down, down, sparkling as it sinks, but ever growing dimmer, dimmer, until I fear that ere I am hardly bemoaning my first grey hairs I shall have to bethink myself to say truly whether indeed I did share in the clash and struggle of a vigorous war; whether indeed I have seen painted red on the sky the tattered flags of Jackson's battalions. No, indeed, I am wrong; that magic name would even in death bear me back in spirit to the clover fields of Virginia, to the Valley and the turnpike, remembering how even *I* followed *him.*

On April 9, 1865, we reached the neighborhood of Appomattox and came to a halt and were drawn up in line. As we marched through a field I saw the Sergeant Major and two other prisoners whom we had taken in tow on the night of the 2nd, now safe in the hands of our prisoner's guard, and as we passed we exchanged greetings. As I remember it, I wished him good treatment in prison and an early exchange and he thanked me in all seriousness, neither recognizing the absurdity of it.

Over to the left, some fighting was going on, and the Sharpshooters were ordered forward. We marched down across an open field to a stream some six yards wide perhaps, crossing on a log thrown across it, and formed on the other side—the enemy's ground. We were about to advance to the attack when, to our surprise, we were recalled. We marched over to the big road, entering it near a house on top of which floated a large yellow flag—the hospital flag.

As we marched up the road toward our Brigade, we saw a queer sight. Through the field, close by the road, a piece of artillery was being driven, and the drivers and artillerymen accompanying it were all Yankees! We didn't understand, but somebody said we had just captured the piece, and its own men were being made to drive it into our lines.

Then I saw a Federal officer come galloping in, carrying aloft a white handkerchief. What did this mean? Had we surrounded a small body of the enemy, and were they about to surrender?

Presently the whisper began to pass from mouth to mouth, that it was a flag of truce, and that *Gen. Lee* was about to surrender. I remember with what surprise and utter discredit I heard the rumor. The thought had never actually entered my mind before, hard pressed as I knew we were. The idea was simply preposterous and I hooted it. There had been surrenders and there would be surrenders, but Gen. Lee's army surrender? Never!

The firing had all ceased, and we saw Confederate regiments returning from the field of battle. And now the whole army—and a small one it was—gathered together on a low hill over against Appomattox. And along the ridge of hills opposite were stretched the long dark lines of the enemy. They lay directly in our front, blocking our further retreat. We were drawn up in column of regiments, I believe, and ordered to stack arms. And then the rumor grew louder and more assured that we were indeed about to surrender.

I took alarm. We were not kept to our pieces, but were let wander about, resting under the trees, and there the enemy was in full view! And no fighting anywhere. I looked up Capt. Barnwell and asked him what he knew. He *knew* nothing, but thought it not improbable that Gen. Lee was about to surrender.

I looked up Gen. McGowan and begged him to tell me whether he knew. He did not know for certain, but—. Then I told him I would not stay if a surrender was to be made. I had been in prison once, and was not going again. I would make my way out and join General Johnston in North Carolina. Gen. McGowan advised me not to act hastily; wait until surrender became certain, then if I would, to go.

I talked with Blackwood. He was ready to follow me anywhere. I did not want many companions, and spoke to only one other. This was Bell—"Old Gator." Yes, he would go with us anywhere—to Texas, if we said so. But 'Gator had a friend, Clarke, who was Bell's neighbor at home. Bell looked up to him and thought very much of him, and could not leave without telling him goodbye. So Bell went off to the wagon train where Clarke was, and Blackwood and I waited. Presently 'Gator returned, tears in his eyes, and declared he could not make up his mind to leave Clarke. As he was in great doubt as to what he ought to do, we all went together to Clarke to talk about it. The upshot of it was that Bell decided to remain with Clarke.

Shortly before this I had gone to Gen. McGowan again to ask whether we were really going to surrender. I had found him in the woods, crying, half-dressed, taking off his old dirty uniform, and putting on a newer brighter one used on state occasions. I did not then need his acknowledgment of our miserable fate. His face and the changing of his uniform were enough.

By that time it had got to be well known among the men that Lee had determined to surrender, and it was a lamentable spectacle to see how the men took it. Some seemed to be glad that it was all over, but even they, I have no doubt, would have been as ready to charge as the rest, had it been so ordered. But mostly there were sad and gloomy faces. For myself, I cried. I could not help it. And all about were men crying— plenty of them. We left Gen. McGowan crying, and Clarke and Bell also.

I had in my pocket two dollars, a greenback bill, which Father had sent me in a letter. Hearing it reported that the terms of surrender stipulated parole for all privates and non-commissioned officers, but that commissioned officers would be sent to Northern prisons, I looked up Capt. Barnwell, and gave him the money. At first he refused to take it. But telling him that he would need it bad enough in prison, I pressed it upon him so that he could not refuse.

So Blackwood and I left the little tattered, weary, sad, and weeping army—*our* army—left them there on the hill with their arms stacked in the field, all in rows—never to see it any more. Telling Clarke and Bell goodbye, we crossed the road into the untenanted fields and thickets, and in a little while lost sight of all that told of the presence of what was left of the army that through four long years, time and again, had beaten back its enemy, keeping Richmond, its capital, safe and sound.

Carrying our rifles, skulking through thick bushes and behind trees, or now crawling along in a ditch to conceal ourselves, now hiding in a fence corner, we at last eluded the vigilance of the enemy's pickets and made good our way out of his lines. Then we set off on our march to join Gen. Johnston in North Carolina.

[EDITORIAL NOTE: When Berry and Blackwood had stolen safely through the Federal picket lines, they headed for Greensboro, North Carolina, intending to join General Johnston's command and continue the fight. They camped in the woods the first night; but discovered next day that when meal time approached they had only to knock on the first door to be cordially invited in and welcomed to share whatever scant fare the house afforded. They usually were offered a bed for the night; but the two boys, ragged and dirty, preferred to accept lodging in the barn.

When in a few days they began to be overtaken by Confederate soldiers, paroled after Lee's surrender and hurrying home, the picture changed somewhat. With so many on the roads, the hospitable citizens were almost "eaten out." Near Danville, they counted themselves lucky, Berry records, "When Mr. George W. Hall gave us something for supper, and we found lodging in a blacksmith shop belonging to Uncle Billy Fry (colored), who gave us a bed of straw." How different from the victorious return these youngsters had often pictured to themselves! But it was comforting that in all this vanquished, bleeding country they were received with gratitude and affection by all from the highest to the most humble.

At Danville they were fortunate to catch a train which took them almost to Greensboro. Arriving at General Johnston's camp April 19th, they were shocked by rumors freely circulated of imminent surrender. On April 22nd, convinced of the accuracy of the rumors, the boys headed for home. They reached their grandfather's house on the White Horse Road, near Greenville, South Carolina, still carrying the rifles which had caused many among the paroled prisoners to remark, "There go two who have not surrendered."

After visiting their grandparents, the boys set out on their final trek homeward, arriving on May 15th. As Augusta had not been in the line of Sherman's march to the sea, it had been spared much of the pillage and destruction visited upon other cities and villages. But it was now under military rule; Federal soldiers garrisoned the city.]